FACULTY BARGAINING IN PUBLIC HIGHER EDUCATION

A Report and Two Essays

A REPORT OF THE CARNEGIE COUNCIL
ON POLICY STUDIES IN HIGHER EDUCATION

A report of the Carnegie Council on Policy Studies in Higher Education

Essays by Joseph W. Garbarino David E. Feller & Matthew W. Finkin

FACULTY BARGAINING IN PUBLIC HIGHER EDUCATION

*A Report
and Two Essays*

 Jossey-Bass Publishers
San Francisco • Washington • London • 1977

FACULTY BARGAINING IN PUBLIC HIGHER EDUCATION
A Report and Two Essays
> The Carnegie Council on Policy Studies in
> Higher Education, Joseph W. Garbarino, David
> E. Feller & Matthew W. Finkin

Copyright © 1977 by: The Carnegie Foundation
for the Advancement of Teaching

> Jossey-Bass, Inc., Publishers
> 615 Montgomery Street
> San Francisco, California 94111

> Jossey-Bass Limited
> 44 Hatton Garden
> London EC1N 8ER

*This report is issued by the Carnegie Council on Policy Studies
in Higher Education with headquarters at 2150 Shattuck Avenue,
Berkeley, California 94704.*

*Copies are available from Jossey-Bass, San Francisco,
for the United States, Canada, and Possessions.
Copies for the rest of the world are available from
Jossey-Bass, London.*

Library of Congress Catalogue Card Number LC 76-50728

International Standard Book Number ISBN 0-87589-322-8

Manufactured in the United States of America

DESIGN BY WILLI BAUM

FIRST EDITION

Code 7721

The Carnegie Council Series

The Federal Role in Postsecondary Education: Unfinished Business, 1975–1980
The Carnegie Council on Policy Studies in Higher Education

More Than Survival: Prospects for Higher Education in a Period of Uncertainty
The Carnegie Foundation for the Advancement of Teaching

Making Affirmative Action Work in Higher Education: An Analysis of Institutional and Federal Policies with Recommendations
The Carnegie Council on Policy Studies in Higher Education

Presidents Confront Reality: From Edifice Complex to University Without Walls
Lyman A. Glenny, John R. Shea, Janet H. Ruyle, Kathryn H. Freschi

Progress and Problems in Medical and Dental Education: Federal Support Versus Federal Control
The Carnegie Council on Policy Studies in Higher Education

Low or No Tuition: The Feasibility of a National Policy for the First Two Years of College
The Carnegie Council on Policy Studies in Higher Education

Managing Multicampus Systems: Effective Administration in an Unsteady State
Eugene C. Lee, Frank M. Bowen

Challenges Past, Challenges Present: An Analysis of American Higher Education Since 1930
David D. Henry

The States and Higher Education: A Proud Past and a Vital Future
The Carnegie Foundation for the Advancement of Teaching

Educational Leaves for Employees: European Experience for American Consideration
Konrad von Moltke, Norbert Schneevoigt

Faculty Bargaining in Public Higher Education: A Report and Two Essays
The Carnegie Council on Policy Studies in Higher Education, Joseph W. Garbarino, David E. Feller, Matthew W. Finkin

Contents

FACULTY BARGAINING IN PUBLIC HIGHER EDUCATION

A Report and Two Essays

A REPORT OF THE CARNEGIE COUNCIL
ON POLICY STUDIES IN HIGHER EDUCATION

Part One

Faculty Collective Bargaining in Public Higher Education— Three Key Issues

Who Decides on Unionization?

What Is Subject to Control Through Collective Bargaining?

Who Is the Employer?

A Report of the Carnegie Council on Policy Studies in Higher Education

Collective bargaining by faculty members in higher education is a development largely of only the past decade—the pioneer City University of New York contract was first signed in 1969. Collective bargaining is, however, already well established:

- 24 states have laws that authorize employees of public institutions of postsecondary education to organize and bargain collectively. (For a list of the 24 states, see Appendix A.) Additionally, 3 states (Illinois, Nevada, and Ohio) and the District of Columbia, by action of governing boards of public institutions of higher education, authorize employees to organize and to bargain collectively if they wish to do so. Employees of private institutions have been similarly covered in all 50 states by the National Labor Relations Act, since the assumption of jurisdiction by the National Labor Relations Board in 1970.
- About 25 percent of the nation's full-time faculty are now included in this form of collective organization, on about 30 percent of the campuses. (For these and other data, see Appendix B, Table 1.)
- In recent years faculty opinion has moved strongly toward greater acceptance of collective bargaining and use of the strike, and toward greater militancy in defending faculty interests. (See Table 1. For additional data on faculty opinions, see Appendix B, Table 2.)

We see no major new circumstances ahead that are likely to change greatly this growing acceptance of collective bargaining.

We state the above as facts. The Council also endorses the view of its predecessor Carnegie Commission on Higher Education that "state laws, where they do not now permit it, should provide faculty members in public institutions the opportunity of obtaining collective bargaining rights."[1]

This is not to recommend, however, that faculty members

[1]Carnegie Commission on Higher Education, *Governance of Higher Education: Six Priority Problems*, April 1973. The Carnegie Commission identified faculty collective bargaining as one of six key issues of governance and institutional management. The Commission recognized and analyzed the underlying economic, political, and socio-cultural factors that were spurring faculties to organize, particularly in community and in specialized four-year colleges lacking strong traditions of faculty authority over issues of academic governance and affected closely by trends toward teacher collective action in elementary and secondary education. The Commission also sponsored two

**Table 1. Faculty opinions about collective bargaining, resort to strikes, and
greater militancy in defending interests**

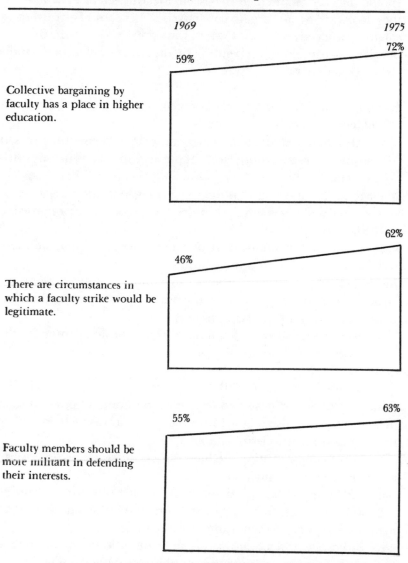

1969   *1975*

                                                                              72%

                              59%

Collective bargaining by
faculty has a place in higher
education.

                                                                              62%

                              46%

There are circumstances in
which a faculty strike would be
legitimate.

                                                                              63%

                              55%

Faculty members should be
more militant in defending
their interests.

Source: Carnegie Commission and Carnegie Council Surveys, 1969 and 1975.

independent research reports and commentaries illuminating the trend toward faculty
organization in higher education: *Faculty Bargaining: Change and Conflict* by Joseph
W. Garbarino in association with Bill Aussieker, McGraw-Hill, New York, 1975; and
Professors, Unions, and American Higher Education by Everett Carll Ladd, Jr., and
Seymour Martin Lipset, Berkeley, 1973.

should necessarily and in all circumstances exercise such rights; nor should they be penalized, as they seem to have been in a few states, if they do not choose to bargain collectively. They should give the most careful consideration, as the Commission pointed out, to the impacts of collective bargaining, depending on the circumstances of the individual situation, on:

Existing formal and informal arrangements for faculty exercise of influence over academic matters

The inclination of students also to organize in response, and to assert pressure at the governing levels of the institution and in the political arena[2]

Managerial authority and attitudes—managerial authority may be increased and managerial attitudes may become more opposed to the faculty

Campus autonomy, public control over higher education, and public attitudes toward higher education

Intercampus and interinstitutional uniformity of policies and practices and, more generally, on tendencies toward centralization, formalization, and rigidification, and

The respective positions of influence of senior and junior faculty members, and of nonfaculty personnel

We also believe that faculty members should give consideration to the potential impacts of collective bargaining, not only on their own interests, but also on the life of the institution as a whole, and on the welfare and attitudes of students.

Collective bargaining can have major consequences for governance, and faculty members should be clear what kind of governance they really want in their particular institution. Collective bargaining is a complex process that can be used by many persons and groups for many ends—some of them quite incompatible.

By now there is enough experience with collective bargaining in higher education to indicate the centrality of these three issues:

[2]See Shark, A. R., Brouder, K., & Associates. *Students and Collective Bargaining* (Washington, D.C.: National Student Educational Fund, 1976).

1. What should be the occupational character and institutional composition of the group of employees that comprise the "election unit" that makes the decision whether or not to bargain collectively through a union with exclusive jurisdiction?
2. Should the "scope of bargaining" be constrained by public legislative or administrative action (as through rulings by a state public employees relations board) or by private actions of the bargaining parties?
3. What institutional or governmental authority shall be legally charged with the obligations and responsibilities of the "employer" for bargaining purposes?

The Council commissioned two complementary studies by nationally recognized scholars of labor law and industrial relations to provide one basis for comment on the policy and administrative aspects of collective bargaining by faculty members[3] in public higher education. Professors David E. Feller of Berkeley and Matthew W. Finkin of Southern Methodist University agreed to define and analyze aspects of collective bargaining of special significance to faculty that present themselves as choices of public policy to be resolved in state enabling legislation. Professor Joseph W. Garbarino of Berkeley agreed to observe, report, and comment critically upon key issues in faculty bargaining as they have emerged in actual practice and in experience with collective bargaining legislation in seven major states.

The Council is pleased to publish these studies in this volume. We have studied carefully the analyses and information they contain in deciding upon principles that we believe should inform and shape policy and practices on the three issues of policy choice in faculty collective bargaining we have set forth above. While we do not always draw the same conclusions as the Feller-Finkin and Garbarino studies, we present them as important investigations of and commentaries upon legislative practice and industrial relations experience as they have developed to date.

---

[3]We do not discuss nonacademic personnel in this report, since there are few if any characteristics that set them aside from employees more generally in regard to collective bargaining.

We set forth below our own conclusions in the three areas we have identified for special consideration. We note that a majority of states (26) do not yet have laws affecting faculty collective bargaining in public institutions of higher education—although only 3 of these 26 (Louisiana, Mississippi, and South Carolina) have not yet considered such legislation; and that the 24 states that do have such legislation may evaluate and revise their laws after a period of operating under them—21 of these 24 have either already amended their laws or have just recently adopted them.[4]

With respect to the three issues (election unit, scope of bargaining, designation of employer) that we consider especially determinative of the impact of bargaining on the values, traditions, and relationships of higher education, a substantial number of existing laws do not include the limiting, prescriptive legislative purpose and language that we consider to be consonant with the needs and best interests of higher education. A report of the Academic Collective Bargaining Information Service (ACBIS)[5] displays the provisions of the various laws on these key issues, state by state. By way of summary, only 7 of the 24 laws explicitly acknowledge "college faculty" as an identifiable employee group covered by the law. Only 4 statutes go beyond "appropriate unit" to define in any detail the nature of the bargaining unit and differentiate between professional and nonprofessional employees. In defining scope of bargaining, 14 state laws go beyond "wages, hours and terms and conditions of employment" by including and/or excluding bargaining subjects; of these, 12 statutes narrow the scope of bargaining by defining "management rights."

---

[4]This status report on state legislation on collective bargaining rests heavily on information and analysis provided by ACBIS, "Analysis of Legislation in 24 States Enabling Faculty Collective Bargaining in Postsecondary Education," *Special Report #17 Update*, May 1976. See also *1976 Update—Collective Bargaining in Education: A Legislator's Guide*, The Education Commission of the States, Denver, January 1976. See also, ACBIS, "Institutions and Campuses with Faculty Collective Bargaining Agents," *Special Report #12 Update*, February 1977; and J. N. Hankin, "State Legislation and the Status of Collective Bargaining in Community and Junior Colleges, 1976," *Special Report #28*, ACBIS, August 1976.

[5]ACBIS, "Analysis of Legislation in 24 States Enabling Faculty Collective Bargaining in Postsecondary Education," *Special Report #17 Update*, May 1976.

Finally, 10 of the 24 state laws name a "special employer" for higher education, distinguishing employment relations in the university from those in other public agencies. In each of these 10 instances, university boards of regents or trustees, or their executive agents, are assigned the obligations and responsibilities of "the employer." Notwithstanding the prescription of law, these "employer" obligations have traditionally been exercised in at least one quite visible state, New York, by the governor's director of the Office of Employee Relations.

We would like to note quickly and emphatically, however, that legislation is not the only way, and sometimes not even the best way, to handle these matters. They may also be resolved (1) by the rulings of the state public employees relations board, (2) by agreement of the parties, or (3) by the actions of individual parties by way of restraint or, conversely, by way of assertion of position. We should also like to note that boards of trustees may take matters into their own hands (as in Illinois, Nevada, Ohio, and the District of Columbia) and authorize collective bargaining on their own. This permits them to set their own rules on the three central issues we have set forth. They can do so in consultation with representatives of their faculties. This makes action through the legislative process unnecessary, allows arrangements that are specific to the special circumstances of institutions of higher education, and reduces the likelihood of political intervention. This is a possibility warranting the most careful consideration.

The Carnegie Council offers its comments on these key issues affecting collective bargaining in higher education from a perception that the nation continues in a dynamic, formative, and experimental period with respect to collective bargaining in the public and eleemosynary sectors of the economy. We believe there are several key policy issues, including the three we have singled out for discussion, that remain essentially undecided.

Our basic concerns, as we survey this range of issues, are (1) to safeguard faculty collegial influence over essential academic matters and (2) to preserve institutional independence from excessive political and governmental control.

1. The Election Unit

The composition of the election unit is of great importance. It constitutes the original building block for collective bargaining.

We wish to distinguish as clearly as we can between the election unit and the bargaining unit. The bargaining unit that negotiates and signs the contract can be, and often is, much larger than the election unit. Election units, of course, should be permitted to join and later withdraw from broader bargaining units if they wish. In New Jersey, for example, each campus individually elected to be represented and then, through coalition, became part of a single statewide bargaining unit.

Two separate issues are involved: (1) the principle of "unions of their own choosing"—best determined by smaller, more homogeneous units of employees that can express most precisely the "consent of the governed" and that can best avoid the "captive" elements that are more likely to be involved in larger and more heterogeneous units and (2) effective bargaining levels and alliances on both the employer's and the union's sides. The first issue is a matter of principle—avoidance, to the extent reasonably possible, of dominance of the opinion of one or more "constituencies" over another unwilling constituency; it is the issue of free choice. The second issue is a matter of power politics—how can power best be asserted on either side? We are here concerned with the first of these issues. To follow the principle of free choice generally leads to smaller, more homogeneous election units. Power considerations, however, frequently lead to larger, more heterogeneous and comprehensive bargaining units.

Our view is that the election unit should be limited to faculty members on an individual campus.[6] We consider this to be the "natural" constituency for determining consent—natural both in terms of common interests and historical practices. We see, as one major exception, a professional school (most likely medicine) that has such a totally separate history and such special problems that its inclusion would be contrary to past practice and to commonality of interests. Some law schools are also in this situation.

We say "faculty members" because they constitute the "colleagues"

---

[6]Other groups of employees on campus are, of course, fully entitled to have their own unit or units.

in the "collegial governance" of academic life. Faculty members are distinguished from other employees, among other ways, in their self-determination over matters of teaching and research; in their sharing of responsibility for department management; in their supervision of other persons, from teaching assistants to secretarial personnel; in their need, because of the special nature of their duties, for special protection for their academic freedom; in their participation in the selection and advancement of their colleagues; in their evaluation of the performances of students and those persons who report to them; in their participation within a national or regional rather than a local labor market; and in their actual or potential coverage by specialized tenure regulations. Faculty members are, in fact, partly employees, partly managers, and partly professional colleagues.

We say "an individual campus" because that is both the historical orientation of faculty members and the face-to-face community to which they feel they belong.

To put it another way, we do not believe that nonfaculty personnel should be able to determine a vote that makes faculty members subject to exclusive representation by a union against their majority will; nor do we believe that votes on another campus or other campuses should bind an unwilling campus into such exclusive representation. We note, in relation to the latter point, that American campuses tend to have individual histories, characteristics, and sets of loyalties that give them a highly prized distinctiveness.

In the normal course of events, almost without question, faculty members would be considered a separate group and the individual campus a separate entity; but, recently, some nonfaculty personnel have begun asserting at least quasi-faculty status, and campuses, often quite diverse in origin and composition, have been placed into systems. These developments have sometimes blurred the underlying realities. .

The introduction of faculty collective bargaining into higher education has coincided with the trend toward confederation and consolidation of individual colleges and universities into broader multicampus institutions and higher education systems for reasons of organizational coherence and managerial control. We believe the intersection of these two dynamic organizational trends has obscured the principles that should determine, on the one hand, the membership characteristics of the group that decides whether or not to organize (the election unit) and, on the other hand, the subsequent organizational arrangement (the bargaining unit) that may best be fitted to represent organized employees in any specific set of negotiations.

As Feller and Finkin point out, most current state statutes make no attempt to limit, through articulation of explicit membership characteristics, the occupational character or geographic scope of the election unit organization. Unfortunately, three of the four states with legislative prescription of the membership characteristics of the election unit (Hawaii, Maine, and Connecticut) mandate either one statewide unit for all faculty, or broad multicampus units for each system of institutions under a common governing board. And the trend of policy via rule making by state public employee relations boards has also been in the direction of larger, more heterogeneous election units, justified on grounds of efficiency, stability, and approximate congruence with that level of public management—the office of the governor or mayor or chairperson of the county board of supervisors—most able to implement agreed-upon arrangements of negotiable matters.

We regret legislative arrangements and trends in administrative rule making that depart from the principle of commonality of professional status and interest with respect to the organization of faculty in higher education institutions. We believe such arrangements are a potential threat to the status and influence of faculty on matters of academic governance, and an active threat to the principle of self-determination and autonomy of individual campus or institutional units.

In contrast, to the maximum practical extent, law and administrative policy should provide for and recognize election unit organizations comprising individuals with common, homogeneous professional and occupational interests, traditions, attitudes, and needs. Homogeneous units provide the most valid barometer of the will of the membership to organize. They also preclude the possibility that the interests of minority subgroups in a multifaceted coalition will be submerged or crudely traded off to advance the claims of more numerous constituent majorities.

Along the lines proposed by Feller and Finkin, we support supplemental arrangements in law or administrative policy that would enable election units established in accord with preferred criteria to merge with other units in a broader structure for bargaining that accords more closely with the scope of institutional or system constituencies actually reached by the issues on the table in any specific negotiation. We similarly support legal arrangements that empower a public employer to demand joint bargaining by two or more employee organizations with respect to matters that have customarily been provided on a uniform basis among the employees thus represented.

The underlying principle is that collective bargaining legislation and administrative rulings should respect and carefully protect the tradition of faculty self-determination in matters of academic organization and management. As Feller and Finkin recommend, enabling legislation should be framed in a way that enables individual faculties to elect whether or not to organize in an election unit organization identical to or congruent with established faculty constituencies and faculty self-governance institutions.

Collective bargaining legislation at the state level should explicitly provide for faculty election units with characteristics that, at a minimum, include:

1. Membership limited to those whose occupational status is defined as membership in the faculty or professoriate, as those terms are used by individual institutions or systems of higher education within the state and
2. Membership limited to eligible faculty members with common relationships to a single institution of higher education, and further limited, where appropriate, to those with common relationships to individual campus or professional units,[7] within a broader, multicampus institution—or at least allow such smaller units to opt out of the process if they so desire

The National Labor Relations Board (NLRB) has had long experience in determining election units, and the states will do well to draw on its experience in this and other respects. In particular, we call attention to the "Globe Doctrine" of the NLRB.[8]

[7]We say this although we recognize the inherent problems involved if, under conditions of rival unionism, two or more units, where the employer is the same, choose different unions as bargaining agents.

[8]Globe Machine and Stamping Co., 3 NLRB 294. This "doctrine" permits "groups

2. The Scope of Bargaining

Currently, most of the statutes authorizing collective bargaining in higher education and other sectors of public employment impose limits on the scope of bargaining by carrying over verbatim, or nearly verbatim, the traditional industrial language focusing on "wages, hours, and terms and conditions of employment." In some statutes, this relatively inclusive language on coverage is complemented with a listing of "management rights" that has the effect of circumscribing those subjects and issues governed by the obligations, procedures, and sanctions of bargaining.

In their lengthy exploration of the theory, law, and experience with various approaches to the question of "coverage" in both the private and public sectors, Professors Feller and Finkin provide substantial evidence of the practical difficulties encountered in trying to use traditional "coverage" language in the basic law to demarcate issues that fall clearly within or beyond the boundary of matters mandatorily subject to bargaining.

If provisions of state enabling legislation and administrative rule making satisfied what Feller and Finkin term the "imperative" condition[9] that faculty election units for representational purposes coincide or correspond closely with established faculty constituencies for purposes of academic governance, we might accept the expansive approach to bargainable issues that they recommend. However, with the trend in law and practice often encouraging or at least permitting large, multidimensional election groups that include but prospectively go well beyond established faculty constituencies for governance, we believe that some other restraints on scope of coverage may be necessary to safeguard established faculty influence on issues of academic governance and management. We say this although we recognize the problem of drafting the necessary legal language (but note that a similar problem also exists in determining what is "mandatory" and what is "permissible"); and we recognize that strong unions have found ways of circumventing definitions of what is

---

of employees with identifiable separate interests" to form their own election unit.

[9]"It is imperative that the faculty's governance constituency coincide with the constituency that selects a bargaining agent if there is to be a satisfactory accommodation between the two" (see p. 111).

"nonpermissible" (but note that faculty unions are not likely to have similar power to flaunt the law).

We believe that, particularly where nonfaculty personnel are included, or where students become part of the bargaining process, or where more than one campus is involved, and especially where the campuses are diverse in history and functions, special legislation or administrative rulings, or other actions, should safeguard the intellectual missions of higher education. Specifically, we believe that collective bargaining should not be permitted to determine:

The selection and conduct of research by individual faculty members
The content of courses and methods of teaching by individual faculty, or the development of programs of study
The selection and promotion to tenure of individual faculty members[10]
The determination of individual student grades and the awarding of individual degrees
The selection of individual academic leadership

These decisions are at the heart of the academic enterprise. They should be made either on the basis of individual judgment or on the basis of collegial wisdom about merit. We believe that collective bargaining should not control scholarly activities and that there should be a sphere of academic autonomy that covers all those processes and decisions that are directly involved in the discovery, the interpretation, and the transmission of knowledge. We also believe that the essential managerial authority of trustees and administrators should be safeguarded so that they are in a position to give general direction and to provide leadership within their own sphere of authority.

We believe that the scope of bargaining in higher education should be limited by legislation, administrative rulings, or by practice to issues that bear directly upon "wages, hours[11] and terms and

[10]With the exception that grievance action should be possible if the administration does not follow the recommendation of the faculty committee on privilege and tenure.

[11]We note the difficulty and the dangers in specifying hours for faculty members. Their duties are quite diverse and often irregular in their timing. Encouragement of a "time-clock" approach would be quite unwise.

conditions of employment"—essentially items that have a monetary dimension—and that those matters that traditionally constitute the essence of "academic freedom and autonomy" should be specifically excluded. We favor their exclusion also from determination by political authorities under any circumstances, and call attention to the fact that political authorities increasingly sit on one side of the bargaining table. The scope of bargaining applies to both sides—the governor, if he is the "employer," as well as the union. The issue is not just what the union may want to bargain about but also what the "employer," however defined, may want to bargain about. Bargaining is a two-way street.

We do not mean to suggest by any of the above that a union in higher education might not bargain about the establishment of an academic senate of faculty members to provide oversight of academic matters, or about general policies and procedure.

The problem is complicated and cannot be solved by reference to "management rights" alone. In addition to "bargaining rights" and "management rights" in higher education, there are also "academic" or "professional" or "collegial rights." Reference to management rights, in fact, may actually reduce academic rights (as in Hawaii) by delegating to a board of trustees or other "employer" those decisions that are or should be made at the faculty level. Our specific preferences are as follows:

1. That, particularly where the "imperative" condition of Feller and Finkin regarding election units is not observed, the law exempt "collegial rights," and make clear that the phrase "management rights" is not intended to reduce faculty influence over "collegial rights"
2. That a state's public employee relations board make these distinctions if the state law confines itself to the usual "wages, hours and terms and conditions of employment" and "management rights" terminology
3. That the parties jointly agree to exempt collegial rights
4. That individual parties act so as to encourage the exemption of collegial rights:
   The academic senate assures that it is a viable and effective unit
   The union exercises restraint in the area of collegial rights

The administration refuses in collective bargaining to agree to a diminution of collegial rights

The governor, if he is involved, exercises restraint in these areas. The legislature also exercises restraint—faculty unions should not be able to gain through legislation what they have failed to secure in collective bargaining

We recognize the problem of defining the excluded areas and of interpreting the definitions, but this problem also exists in connection with "mandatory" areas for bargaining, as we have noted above, and the laws involved have universally set forth what is mandatory.

We make these comments because in the history of collective bargaining resultant agreements tend to cover a wider and wider range of topics over a period of time.[12] Unions press for an extension of bargaining rights while management seeks to protect management rights; as a result, in higher education, there might be no one at the bargaining table in a position to protect collegial rights unless one or more of the actions suggested above is taken.[13]

3. The Employer

Authorities on the functioning of collective bargaining in the private sector have traditionally argued that the party to a negotiation functioning as "employer" must be in position to deliver the resources required to carry out the negotiated agreement. With the introduction of collective bargaining in the public sector, this truism of traditional labor-management relations has led political chief executives—par-

[12]In a study of practice in 14 states, it was found that almost all issues raised by unions have been held "mandatory" or "permissible" for the employees to negotiate, and that virtually the only issues ruled to be "nonpermissible" have been those where the law already specifically determines the issue—with this one exception, the excluded nonpermissible category is essentially empty of content. (See ACBIS, "Scope of Public Sector Bargaining in 14 Selected States," *Special Report #25 Update*, January 1977.) The California law (the Rodda Act), covering community college faculty members, adds another category of items—those on which the union may "consult"—including "the definition of educational objectives, the determination of the content of courses and curriculum, and the selection of textbooks."

[13]In a famous German case, the judicial system finally had to step in to protect collegial rights from tripartite determination. (*Urteil des Bundesverfassungsgerichts vom 29 Mai 1973—1BvR 424/71—1BvR 325/72—in dem Verfahren über die Verfassungsbeschwerde von 398 Professoren gegen das Vorschaltgesetz für ein Niedersächsisches Gesamthochschulgesetz vom 26 October 1971.*)

ticularly governors—to seek authority for, and equip themselves with, specialized staff to act as the employer in labor negotiations covering the varied jurisdictions of their geopolitical domain.

But here again, in higher education, we have an in-between situation—just as in the three-fold distinction among bargaining, management, and collegial rights—that does not fit the standard rules. In industry, the employer has the resources; in state government, the governor has the resources. In higher education, the resources come from mixed sources. Generally in public higher education the percentage distribution of total institutional resources by source is as follows:

States	52
Federal government	22
Tuition	9
Localities	7
Other sources, including gifts	10

These proportions, of course, vary greatly from institution to institution. State agencies, by contrast, are usually supported entirely by state resources. Who then should be the "employer" where there are diverse sources of funds and where the institution is state-supported but not state operated?

Historically, the general organizational status of public higher education has been legally and politically handled as a special case. This practice continues, to some extent, in the era of collective bargaining. As noted earlier, while collective bargaining legislation is, in general, nonprescriptive and permissive with respect to the special jurisdiction of higher education, the statutes in 10 of the more active states explicitly designate educational rather than political authorities, at the institutional or statewide level, to exercise the authority and responsibilities of the employer.

As Professor Garbarino notes in his monograph, however, the recognized inability of educational authorities to deliver the full resources required to carry out a negotiated agreement without recourse to supplemental consultations and ultimate approval by such political authorities as the governor and state legislature introduces into all negotiations conducted on this basis weakness, uncertainty, and tentativeness that, in specific situations, may call into question the seriousness, usefulness, or validity of the collective bargaining process.

The problems inherent in making an intermediate educational authority the employer for purposes of bargaining lead Professor Garbarino to endorse the practice increasingly engaged in by New York and New Jersey, where representatives of the governor, notwithstanding the provisions of the law, substitute for educational authorities in negotiating contracts with faculty and other educational employees, and in defending, justifying, explaining, and lobbying for approval and funding of the terms of these arrangements in the legislature.

We acknowledge the appeal of an apparently evolving practice that goes some distance toward closing the gap between educational authorities that bargain as management and the political authorities that ultimately determine which educational costs shall be satisfied. In our view, however, the practice evolving in New York and elsewhere directly and unacceptably invites, or at least permits, intervention by political authority into issues of institutional management and academic affairs. Under the New York model, authority for institutional and systems management, including budget and finance, will increasingly be shared and inescapably blurred, in our view, between educational and political authorities.

Since resources for the support of higher education in any given year in any given legislature are not infinitely flexible or elastic, the New York model permits political authority, in the institution of the legislature, to make crude trade-offs between contract increments, on the one hand, and an institution's ongoing base program and budget, on the other. In contrast, when hard financial trade-offs are required, we believe they should be defined and implemented by academic management, not by political authority, with full utilization of established procedures for faculty consultation, participation, and decision-making. We recognize that the governor and the legislature in New York have shown great restraint thus far, but their counterparts have not always done so, particularly in Hawaii, and there are constant temptations to intervene. Thus, we agree with Professor Garbarino on the historical trend, on the powerful attraction of the governor's office for those seeking money, and on the simplicity of the solution, but we question the long-term desirability of this approach.

We consider bargaining arrangements in Michigan a preferable model. Here, the institutional leader and his board are responsible for presenting, defending, lobbying for, and ultimately living with appropriations made available by the legislature and governor for the conduct of higher education, including the payment of wages and salaries agreed upon through a bargaining process. If incremental appropriations are not sufficient to cover the cost of an agreed-upon contract, the institutional leadership is obligated and expected to find resources elsewhere, either through retrenchment or through tuition or other revenue increases. To make this approach workable, the board needs to have control over such matters as tuition levels and internal transfer of funds. The Michigan model will work best, of course, where the institutions of higher education have substantial autonomy. It will apply least well—and is not a viable alternative— where centralized state authority is already well established.

While these arrangements create a dichotomy of a sort between the educational authority that bargains as employer and the political authority that ultimately provides the state appropriations, it is a dichotomy that does not erode the final managerial prerogatives and responsibilities of the academic leader and the board. It is also a dichotomy whose existence can be minimized, where it is not eliminated, by educational leadership with skill and clarity in its relationships with political authority.

We recognize that most actual situations lie between the New York and the Michigan models, with both the governor and the board involved in negotiations. Potentials for misunderstandings over responsibilities are inherent in such arrangements.

In defining or designating an authority or agent to assume the responsibilities of the employer in collective bargaining proceedings, state enabling legislation, we believe, should strive to safeguard the tradition of maximum institutional autonomy, leadership and control in the management of academic programs and all resources that are involved in their provision. State enabling legislation should designate the governing board of each individual institution, or "systems" group of consolidated institutions, to serve as the employer for its sphere of higher education in collective bargaining proceedings, allowing it to designate its bargaining representatives—normally the president or someone reporting to him. In addition, collective bargaining legislation should reinforce the unencumbered authority of the designated employer to manage such financial resources as political authorities may appropriate to fulfill the employer's obligations under negotiated settlements with higher education employees.

Specifically, we do not believe that governors or legislatures, either through collective bargaining or in its absence, should determine:

Assignment of funds to specific purposes
Appointment and promotion of individual faculty members
Determination of specific salaries
Determination of individual workloads or of specific assignments to faculty and staff members
Policies on and administration of research and service activities
Policies on size and rate of growth of departments and schools and colleges within general budgetary limitations
Design of individual buildings and internal assignment of space within general policies—for example, on energy conservation
Specific academic programs for new campuses and other major new endeavors within general authorization by the legislature and within established policies on differentiation of functions
Development of and detailed planning for innovation

We recognize that some institutional presidents (and some boards) accept or even welcome political authorities becoming the employer, for this allows the presidents (or the boards) to avoid many responsibilities and hard decisions and permits them to assume the more popular role, at least in the short run, of "business agent" for campus constituencies, passing along all requests. The president should, of course, represent the members of his institution, but he should also select what he presents, help to reconcile opposing points of view, make decisions, and take responsibility. Otherwise political authorities can become presidents by default, the powers of the president can be seriously eroded, academic autonomy can be unduly circumscribed, and political intrusions into academic decision making can be made easy. The president should not only represent members of the institution. He should also defend. The best defense is effective and responsible leadership. Unwise political intrusions into academic independence can, of course, occur in the absence of collective bargaining; but collective bargaining, unless properly structured, can become a means for such intrusions rather than a barrier against them.

Our preferences are as follows:

1. That the governing board be established as the employer.
2. If the governor is to be directly involved, that there be two-tier bargaining, with money matters bargained with the governor and nonmoney matters with the board, or three-tier bargaining in multicampus systems, with some local nonmoney matters bargained about at the campus level.
3. If the governor negotiates the total agreement, that he exercise restraint in accepting or asserting as bargainable items those matters that do not affect the budget of the state, as most governors thus far have done.
4. In the case of both (2) and (3) above, that the budget requests of the state be divided between the "basic" budget and "additive" personnel costs, with the additive personnel costs being subject to bargaining by the union and with the basic budget subject to handling by the board with the governor and legislature. In any event, the governor as "employer" should consult closely with the executive leaders of higher education.
5. In the case of (1) above, some items may need to be left open until the state budget has been adopted. The union should, of course, be free to assist the board to obtain the state funds necessary to fund the agreement. We note that, even when the governor negotiates an agreement, it cannot take effect until the legislature has appropriated the money. Completion of the contract should be subject, as is often the case, to "availability of financial resources."

Our three recommendations, taken together, are designed to assure (1) that unions really be of "their own choosing," as was the purpose of the original Wagner Act establishing the National Labor

Relations Board, (2) that academic authorities control academic matters, and (3) that campus (and system) autonomy be guarded carefully. Failing these assurances, one campus or group of campuses can determine an important aspect of the fate of another campus against its will; one group or groups of nonacademic employees can, again against the will of those directly concerned, affect the academic conduct of faculty members; academic matters can be placed under nonacademic, nonprofessional control; and the academic enterprise can be gradually transformed into civil service.

In making our comments we recognize that the trend to date in higher education, and over a longer period of time outside higher education, is to move in directions other than those which we recommend: toward more comprehensive election and bargaining units; toward more comprehensive agreements; toward negotiations at the highest possible level. We believe, however, that higher education should set its own distinctive pattern because (1) faculty members are partly managers, partly employees, and partly professional colleagues, (2) collegial rights must be considered as well as the usual bargaining rights and management rights, (3) academic institutions in the public segment are neither state agencies nor self-supporting private businesses but have several sources of support and several reference groups they must consider, and (4) academic institutions have a mixed form of governance.

Much is at stake. The early decisions by governors, legislatures, state public employee relations boards, boards of trustees, presidents, and faculties can help determine the historical axis of development for a long time to come. We recognize that any system of arrangements can be made to work, but we are concerned with what system has the best chance of working well in the long run. This involves, among other things, protecting academic influence over academic matters and safeguarding essential institutional independence from government domination.

William Bowen
President
Princeton University

Nolen M. Ellison
President
Cuyahoga Community College

Appendix A

**Twenty-four states enabling faculty collective bargaining
in public postsecondary education**

Alaska (1972)
California (1975, 2-year institutions only)
Connecticut (1975)
Delaware (1970)
Florida (1974)
Hawaii (1973)
Iowa (1974)
Kansas (1970, 2-year institutions; and 1974)
Maine (1974, Vocational and Technical only; and 1975)
Massachusetts (1974)
Michigan (1973)
Minnesota (1974)
Montana (1975)
Nebraska (1972)
New Hampshire (1975)
New Jersey (1974)
New York (1967)
Oregon (1975)
Pennsylvania (1970)
Rhode Island (1973)
South Dakota (1973)
Vermont (1975)
Washington (1973, 2-year institutions only)
Wisconsin (1974, Vocational and Technical only)

Source: Based on ACBIS, "Analysis of Legislation in 24 States Enabling Faculty Collective Bargaining in Postsecondary Education," *Special Report #17 Update*, May 1976.

Appendix B

Table 1. A statistical profile of collective bargaining in public postsecondary education—1977: campuses with faculty collective bargaining agents

	Four-year		Two-year		Four-year and two-year combined	
	Number of campuses	Percent of public campuses in state	Number of campuses	Percent of public campuses in state	Number of campuses	Percent of national total
Alaska			9	100	9	1.8
California			9	9	9	1.8
Connecticut	10	100	16	100	26	5.5
Delaware	1	50	4	100	5	1.0
District of Columbia	2	100	1	100	3	0.6
Florida	13	100	4	14	17	3.5
Hawaii	2	100	7	100	9	1.8
Illinois	5	39	21	45	26	5.4
Iowa	1	33	19	90	20	4.1
Kansas	1	13	9	42	10	2.1
Maine			6	100	6	1.2
Maryland	1	8	2	12	3	0.6
Massachusetts	10	67	15	79	25	5.1
Michigan	9	60	31	100	40	8.2
Minnesota	7	64	18	90	25	5.1
Montana	3	50	2	67	5	1.0
Nebraska	5	63	11	100	16	3.3
New Jersey	14	100	16	100	30	6.2
New York	37	93	44	100	81	16.6
Ohio	11	85			11	2.3
Oregon	1	13	8	62	9	1.8
Pennsylvania	17	74	14	36	31	6.4
Rhode Island	2	100	1	100	3	0.6
Vermont	3	75	1	50	4	0.8
Washington			23	85	23	4.7
Wisconsin	1	8	38	97	39	8.0
Outlying Areas (Guam)	1	100			1	0.2
Total	157	25	329	35	486	100.0

Source: Based on ACBIS, "Institutions and Campuses with Faculty Collective Bargaining Agents," *Special Report #12 Update*, February 1977.

Table 2. Faculty opinions about collective bargaining: in 1969 and 1975

	Collective bargaining has a place in higher education (percentage agree)[a]		There are circumstances in which a faculty strike would be legitimate (percentage yes)[b]		Faculty members should be more militant in defending their interests (percentage agree)[c]	
	1969	1975	1969	1975	1969	1975
All faculty	59	72	46	62	55	63
Type of institution						
Research Universities I	53	64	46	59	56	61
Research Universities II	53	65	43	59	53	63
Doctoral Universities I	56	69	45	61	55	61
Doctoral Universities II	58	66	47	58	58	61
Comprehensive Univs. & Colleges I	63	74	49	62	57	67
Comprehensive Univs. & Colleges II	66	78	48	66	57	68
Liberal Arts Colleges I	57	70	45	66	52	62
Liberal Arts Colleges II	61	72	45	58	53	59
Two-Year Colleges	68	82	47	67	53	63
Self-described political leaning						
Left	88	92	93	91	90	90
Liberal	68	80	61	74	68	76
Middle of the road	55	70	37	57	47	59
Strongly or moderately conservative	45	58	26	45	38	46
Evaluation of personal salary level						
Excellent	48	63	38	52	47	53
Good	55	65	42	56	51	55
Fair	63	74	50	64	59	66
Poor	73	79	61	71	67	74

Evaluation of effectiveness of
faculty senate

Excellent	52	63	35	53	42	49
Good	55	67	39	54	47	52
Fair	61	71	48	59	56	61
Poor	67	75	59	69	70	73

Evaluation of administration

Excellent	46	54	30	40	38	38
Good	55	65	39	52	47	52
Fair	63	74	52	64	62	66
Poor	73	79	67	74	76	79

[a] Percentage responding "disagree strongly" or "disagree with reservations" that "collective bargaining by faculty members has no place in a university."

[b] 1969 = Percentage responding "definitely yes" or "probably yes" that "there are circumstances in which a strike would be a legitimate means of collective action for faculty members."
1975 = Percentage responding "strongly agree" or "agree with reservations."

[c] 1969 and 1975 = Percentage responding "strongly agree" or "agree with reservations."

Source: Carnegie Commission and Carnegie Council Surveys, 1969 and 1975.

Part Two

State Experience
in Collective Bargaining

Joseph W. Garbarino

Professor of Business Administration
Director of the Institute of Business and
*   Economic Research*
University of California, Berkeley

1

Overview

Faculty unionism first came to national attention when the faculty of the City University of New York (CUNY) chose a bargaining agent at the end of 1969. Seven years later, faculty collective bargaining was established in about 430 institutions of higher education and covered approximately 120,000 faculty and professional staff, or about one of four faculty members. Two-thirds of the represented faculty are to be found in four-year colleges and 90 percent of the total are in public institutions. After two years of slow growth in 1973 and 1974, the pace of expansion quickened in 1975 and continued to accelerate in 1976.

In this analysis, the emphasis will be on the administrative aspects of the new bargaining arrangements in four-year colleges and universities. Although more attention has probably been directed to the academic issues, faculty bargaining has so far created more change in administrative structures and procedures than it has in academic affairs. In the long run, of course, the key question is how the developments in administrative relationships can be expected to affect academic matters.[1]

---

[1] A note on methodology: Although the author has been working in this area since 1970, most of this discussion is based on material collected during visits made to the states of New York, New Jersey, Pennsylvania, Massachusetts, Rhode Island, Michigan, and Hawaii in 1975 with some follow-up in 1976. These states include about 80 percent of all represented faculty. Attention was concentrated on public four-year institutions and on system and state relations. Approximately 60 interviews were conducted. Some mail and telephone inquiries sampled experience in Ohio and Delaware. The monograph *Faculty Bargaining, State Government and Campus Autonomy*, edited

At this time a review of academic unionism suggests that five of the most important problem areas are:

1. Bargaining structure and the identity of the employer
2. Bargaining and the budget process
3. The organized students' role in faculty bargaining
4. Bargaining in multi-institutional systems
5. Bargaining units and internal institutional administration

In Chapter One I shall try to summarize the results of my review of bargaining experience on each of these questions. In Chapter Two I shall take up each issue in turn and discuss them in detail.

Bargaining Structure and the Identity of the Employer

A remarkable diversity of bargaining patterns prevails in the seven states studied. In one state, Hawaii, bargaining is carried out by an agency of the state for all higher education in a single negotiation. In two others, Michigan and Massachusetts, bargaining is decentralized to the individual institutions or systems of institutions. In three states, New York, New Jersey, and Pennsylvania, a mixed system has developed, with some public institutions bargaining largely on their own, while other negotiations are conducted by a state agency. Finally, in Rhode Island bargaining is conducted by a member of the staff of the board of trustees, with each segment of higher education separately, but with direct and close coordination with the office of the governor. In short, in five of the seven states the office of the governor has a direct influence on the bargaining process in all or a major part of higher education in the state. This represents perhaps the most important single administrative change that faculty bargaining has introduced into higher education.

Although the potential for direct intervention into the academic substance of bargaining by the governor's office clearly exists, this development does not seem to have created major problems in the relations between the executive branch and the central headquarters

---

by Kenneth Mortimer and published by the Education Commission of the States (1976) was very helpful, particularly the papers by Mortimer, Kenneth Lau, James Begin, and William Weinberg.

of the systems. (A possible qualification to this statement by the presidents of the units of multi-institutional systems will be discussed below.) This seems to be the result of the relatively narrow scope of the bargaining that has taken place and the relatively low priority given to higher education problems in these states in recent years. State executives have not felt impelled to implement major changes in state-higher education policy, and they have been willing to act as agents for the educational administrators of their states without attempting to introduce major initiatives of their own. The states' interests in the collective bargaining process in higher education have been financial rather than educational.

Whether the governor's office or the educational institutions function as the employer in the conduct of bargaining has a great impact on the financing of the collective bargaining settlements. I therefore combine my recommendations on bargaining structure with those on financing at the end of the next section on the budget process.

Bargaining and the Budget

At the time of my interviews, every state visited except Hawaii was undergoing a budgetary crisis. Even if one assumes that the severity of the crises was unusual, it is clear that the financial problems will persist for a substantial period.

From the point of view of college or university administrators, the preferred arrangement would be for the separate institutions to control their bargaining, with any settlement reached going into effect only when and if the costs of any concessions were covered by appropriations made specifically for that purpose and without reference to the overall institutional budget. This situation does not exist anywhere, although something like it could evolve in Massachusetts. The worst situation from the institution's point of view would be to have someone else negotiate the contract without taking the responsibility for financing the settlement. Fortunately, this situation does not exist in its pure form either.

The two extremes of current practice are exemplified by New York and Massachusetts. In New York the Office of Employee Relations negotiates the State University of New York (SUNY) contract, and the bargaining law provides that contracts do not become effective until the legislature provides the funds required. The money has been provided as an appropriation separate from the institutional budget as a whole. The Massachusetts system was tried for the first time in 1975; until then economic issues had not been negotiable. Each institution (for example, Southeastern Massachusetts University) or each system (for example, the state college system) has been negotiating with their unions separately, with the resulting contracts submitted directly to the legislature for action. Southeastern Massachusetts University was reported to have had a proposed contract before a legislative committee since January 1975. As of October 1976 no action had been taken on funding the contracts in higher education.

One prediction is that the Massachusetts legislature will delay on all contracts until the pattern for other state employees is established and will then provide an equivalent settlement for higher education. If institutions negotiate contracts with their unions that call for more benefits, they will have to deal with the problem themselves either by renegotiating them or funding the costs from other sources.

The Massachusetts system will probably evolve toward the Michigan pattern, in which each institution bargains its own contract and is responsible for its financing. Each Michigan institution submits its own budget as a whole through the governor's office and follows it through the legislature. The institution knows it has to live with the joint results of its union bargaining and its legislative lobbying within the confines of its general budget.

In my opinion, despite its dangers, the New York approach as it has worked to date provides the best combination of bargaining arrangements likely to be attained by higher education. The state functions as the employer/negotiator but appears to have had little independent influence on the academic content of the contracts. The economic provisions of the contract settlement itself have not come into effect until the legislature has provided funds, the governor has been committed to the resulting agreement, and the funding problem has been handled independently of the general budget for the institution.

It is axiomatic that those negotiating the contract ought to be responsible for its financing. Unfortunately, no structural arrangements can ensure this result in public employee bargaining. Arrangements in Pennsylvania that appear on their face to follow the New York pattern seem to be disintegrating under the pressures of financial stringency. Nevertheless, in designating the employer for bargaining purposes, the principle of linking the responsibility for negotiations and financing is a sound one and should be followed.

Students and the Bargaining Process

Any discussion of student participation in faculty collective bargaining triggers an emotional reaction from all parties.

A point to be stressed at the outset is that there has been very little actual experience with student participation in faculty negotiations in four-year colleges, although two states (Oregon and Montana) have now provided for such participation in their laws. The degree of student participation in the highly publicized Massachusetts State College negotiations has been greatly exaggerated in popular discussion. Until 1975 bargaining in Massachusetts was on noneconomic matters and, with the introduction of bargaining on economic issues this year, this experiment has ended in the minority of colleges in which it had been in effect.

More important, the current experience with bargaining during a financial crisis suggests that much of the student concern with participation is misdirected.[2] Most of the threats to student interests are not being generated in the collective bargaining negotiations themselves, but in the budgetary decisions that are necessary to finance the settlements and other cost increases. As an example, Wayne State, facing a $6 million deficit in 1975–76, planned on making up two-thirds of this amount by unilateral tuition increases and cuts in operating budgets. The remaining one-third was being negotiated with the union, with some combination of reduced pay increases and reduction in staff as the proposed solution. Unless all management budgetary decisions are to be included in the scope of bargaining, most of the impact of the financing decisions on students would be beyond the reach of any form of participation in faculty-administration negotiations. One of the neglected considerations in proposals to include stu-

2On balance, an excellent case can be made that student participation in governance, as distinct from negotiations, has been expanded as unions and administrations have made concessions in governance areas to avoid including students in bargaining.

dents is that the addition of parties to the process makes any attempt to limit the scope of bargaining more difficult.

So far as the effect of faculty bargaining agreements on students is presumed to be generated by cost pressures, students have nearly as much reason to be involved in the institutions' negotiations with nonacademic employees or with the finance committees of legislatures.

Many faculty demands, such as those affecting workload and the continuation of programs, have beneficial side effects for students, but in general the protection of students' interests should be the concern of the administration. Usually students will find that most decisions affecting their welfare are made as part of the general budgetary process, away from the bargaining table. Student participation in faculty bargaining is likely to make reaching agreement between the principals more difficult and to contribute to factionalism and instability in the internal affairs of faculty unions.

Student governments or other student organizations are likely to develop a form of bilateral bargaining with administrations to protect their interests. It would be a serious mistake to give these arrangements formal status in law and thereby encourage the growth of formal student representation in negotiations, as proposed in some states, notably Massachusetts.

Bargaining and Multi-Institutional Systems

Collective bargaining by faculty is highly concentrated in large multi-institutional systems. SUNY and CUNY are by far the largest, but other organized systems include the universities of Florida and Hawaii, and the Pennsylvania, New Jersey, Nebraska, and Minnesota state college systems. Some of the problems associated with systems that are single bargaining units also appear in systems whose central administration conducts separate negotiations with single institutions, as in the Massachusetts state colleges.

Collective bargaining in a multi-institutional system of higher education seems to maximize the effect of bargaining on nonfinancial issues. Although conflicts arise between central administrations and the state agencies that usually control the bargaining, the greatest concern with the results of bargaining is found internally, in its effects on the relations between central administrations and the administrations on the separate campuses.

Although a good deal of coordination and consultation between the central offices and the separate campuses is typical, local administrations feel that bargaining has contributed to a shift of authority and initiative in a wide variety of matters either to the central administration of the systems or to the educational agencies in the state capitols. Campus presidents sometimes seem to regard central administrations and the state bureaucracy as natural allies who are tempted to use collective bargaining as an opportunity to accumulate power at central headquarters at the expense of the local administrations.

Faculty bargaining is only one of many forces behind the apparent drift of power to the state capitols. Increased coordination and control of policy in higher education is a trend that has been noted for many years. Faculty collective bargaining can contribute to the trend toward centralization with or without an explicit policy on the part of the system administration.

In one state, an official in the negotiating unit referred to collective bargaining as a "management tool" of the central administration. Bargaining at system headquarters exerts pressure toward a uniform policy on the issues covered and permits direct system intervention into such matters as teaching evaluation and salary administration at the campus level. Whether this intervention is a benefit or a detriment depends on the situation as well as the point of view of the evaluator. In general, my opinion is that administrative convenience is likely to weigh too heavily in the considerations of system officials and that a policy of administrative self-denial is desirable to maintain campus diversity and independence. Experiments with two-tier bargaining—with local administration and local union bargaining on noneconomic issues while economic questions are handled in higher-level negotiations—have been tried in Massachusetts and New Jersey, and this approach ought to be encouraged. The pattern of national negotiations at central headquarters coupled with supplementary local agreements is well established in private sector bargaining, and a version appropriate to higher education should be developed.

Bargaining Units and Internal Administration

This category is something of a catch-all for issues arising out of internal administrative problems. The three problems identified are those involving unions of graduate students, unions of "middle management," and the agency shop issue.

In institutions with substantial graduate programs the question of dealing with graduate student unions may arise, whether or not the faculties unionize. Where the faculties are unorganized (for example, Michigan and Wisconsin) the problem is one of institutional bargaining strategy and of the requirements of state law. Where there are unions of faculty on campus (for example, CUNY and Rutgers), the question arises of whether the organized students and faculty should be in separate units or combined. I could find no instance in which separate unions of employed graduate students and faculty have been recognized as exclusive bargaining agents for their constituents on a single campus. At CUNY the employed graduate students are members of the unit. When the issue arose at Rutgers, the American Association of University Professors (AAUP) faculty unit accepted the students as members of the unit, with administration encouragement. The students make up over 30 percent of the unit. Students do not seem to have added any particular problems to the already long list of problems in the CUNY-union relationship. At Rutgers both the bargaining and the internal politics of the union have been made more difficult by the inclusion of students.

In addition to differences in bargaining agenda that result from combining the two groups, employed students and faculty have an employer-employee relationship in many cases. Their inclusion in the same bargaining unit appears to be undesirable.

The question of middle management unions raises some of the same issues, but the more important question here is one of managerial role. Separate unions of management personnel are appearing more frequently and, particularly in Michigan, show signs of affiliating with such nonteaching unions as the United Auto Workers (UAW). The university may well evolve into a collection of organized groups facing a shrinking cadre of "top management" across the bargaining table. This is a problem common to all public employment, and it may be insoluble without support from legislation limiting rights of supervisors in the bargaining process.

Finally, the question of the agency shop, the compulsory payment of a service fee to the union, is growing in importance. In addition to the philosophical objections to compulsion, the principal problem is the relation of tenure and academic freedom to the agency shop when the payment of the service fee is made a condition of employment. A new method of enforcing the agency shop that does not depend on terminating employment has been developed, and, if it withstands legal challenges, may mitigate the problem from the employers' point of view. At Central Michigan and Youngstown State Universities enforcement of the agency shop is not the responsibility of the employer. The employer and the union include an agency shop requirement in the contract, but its enforcement is left up to the union which is expected to use the threat of a civil suit for nonpayment to force individuals to comply.

Faculty unions, like other unions, strongly favor the agency shop and will demand it once they are sure of strong majority support in their unit. University administrations will probably adopt the most common employer strategy in this issue, that of resisting until a high level of voluntary membership is achieved and then granting the type represented by the civil suit variation.

2

State
Experience

Of the five areas summarized in Part One, the first two—involving the structure of bargaining and the financing of settlements—are most important for state-institution relations. In this part of the report, therefore, I shall analyze the experience of each of the major states with regard to these two questions.

Identity of the Employer and Budgeting Arrangements

New York. The two major systems of public higher education that include the four-year institutions in New York State bargain independently of one another. (Both systems include some two-year institutions as well.) Negotiations for SUNY are conducted by the governor's Office of Employee Relations (OER), and the contract that results is signed by the director of the office. Prior to and during negotiations committees are set up to secure information about issues, to study particular problem areas, and in general to bring the constituent institutions into the negotiation process. The OER conducts negotiations for all other state employees, and the SUNY salary adjustments reflect the need for keeping settlements more or less in line between these groups. (In 1975 a substantial discrepancy developed because the faculty contract called for a substantial increase in the second year of a two-year contract negotiated in 1974, while state employees got a much smaller increase in a new contract negotiation.) SUNY faculty are represented by the United University Professions, a union that resulted from the merger of the National Education Association (NEA) and the American Federation of Teachers (AFT) affiliates in New York State. CUNY is represented by the Professional Staff Congress, the product of a similar merger. Recently both unions have severed the tie with the NEA.

New York law provides that all contracts are effective only after the legislature approves the economic elements and that the governor must introduce appropriation bills to accomplish this. Until the two-year contract negotiated in 1974, salaries had been negotiated annually, and the combination of lengthy negotiations and the need for legislative action produced repeated delays in implementing settlements. The New York approach has separated the process of preparing the overall budget from that of financing annual salary adjustments. The overall budget is prepared on the basis of current salaries and the results of negotiations are embodied in separate legislative action at a later date. To date the adequacy of the supplementary appropriations to finance the negotiated settlements has not been an issue.

The advantages of the SUNY system to both parties are substantial. The governor's office is able to relate settlements in different branches of state service to one another. The university has participated in negotiations between OER and the union while not bearing the full burden of confrontation. The questions of the overall university budget and of the financing of the current-year increase for faculty salaries have been separated.

For the university administration, the major problem with this system is that the control of actual negotiations by the state might result in the erosion of its ability to decide questions of academic policy. Up to now this does not seem to have been a problem, but the potential remains.

In my opinion, the decision to negotiate a two-year wage settlement in 1974 was unfortunate because it could threaten the separation of the financing of current settlements from the overall budget process. The 7 percent increase in salary costs scheduled for the second contract year was out of line with other settlements being negotiated for 1975 in one-year contracts with other state employees. Because it would have been very difficult to challenge the implementation of the SUNY settlement, cost pressures created by this increase tended to produce pressures to offset them by reductions in the general university budget for that year. In other words, the financing of the 1975 pay increase without challenge may establish a linkage between the two budgetary procedures in the future, which would reduce one of the major advantages of this approach.

On balance, however, the SUNY system has worked well up to the present time. (Some faculty at SUNY seem to be concerned with the "weakness" of the union exhibited in recent negotiations, but the adaptations to the present budget crisis that might have occurred in the absence of a union might well have been considerably less favorable to the faculty position.) Ideally, the university would be better off controlling its own negotiations, but there is no evidence that negotiators have encroached on university prerogatives, and the university appears to have enjoyed benefits of the system without appreciable cost.

The CUNY system has operated in a quite different fashion, with the Board of Higher Education in New York City functioning as the employer. Although the city has an Office of Collective Bargaining of its own that operates independently of the state's Office of Employee Relations, the Board of Higher Education has controlled negotiations with general coordination with the mayor's office on fiscal limits. The university administration has been the key factor in determining negotiating strategy, with the board functioning in a policy-making role through a system of committees. The board was recently reorganized and expanded to include representatives appointed by the governor's office and a new chairman has been named.

In the 1975 negotiations the new board took a more independent and activist stance in relation to the university administration. The union at CUNY felt that the new board would produce more cooperative attitudes. The vice-chancellor responsible for negotiations with the faculty union resigned in mid-summer during negotiations. As of mid-1975 the then board chairman stated that the members appointed by the governor had not produced a division into blocs on the board. While this may have been true as far as faculty bargaining was concerned, there was general agreement that one of the goals of the state was to introduce tuition at CUNY. The situation at CUNY changed drastically during the municipal budget crisis and the independent effects of faculty bargaining on university affairs have been overwhelmed in the process.

One decision that appears to have come from the city administration was the abandonment of the practice of "indexing" faculty salaries at CUNY by having them tied to those in the lower schools. This tie was broken as a result of negotiation for the first contract in 1970. In spite of the public attention drawn to the level of CUNY salaries, the administration reports that the current highest salary of $33,475 would have been well over $40,000 if indexing had not been replaced by bargaining over salaries. University policy on such matters as open admissions and affirmative action were obviously strongly influenced by the city administration, but these were not implemented through collective bargaining.

In the context of the current crisis in municipal affairs it is difficult to evaluate the collective bargaining experience at CUNY. Before the crisis it appears that bargaining contributed to a greater politicization of decision-making in CUNY because it exacerbated tensions between the board, the university administration, and the faculty. In view of the long history of faculty organization prior to formal unionization and the difficult economic and social conditions involved, it is impossible to separate out the independent effects of unionization, but certainly the impact of the situation on the faculty would have been different in the absence of a union.

In summary, the SUNY arrangements for bargaining have worked well so far as bargaining strucutre and the financing of settlements have been concerned. Bargaining at CUNY has been marked by conflict, but it did not bring either the city or the state administration directly into university academic affairs, at least prior to the present crisis. New York's experience with SUNY is more relevant to other states and New York's approach has been generally successful in that system.

Michigan. Michigan, along with Massachusetts, represents the opposite end of the spectrum of bargaining structure from New York. Collective bargaining in higher education in Michigan is unique in the degree of independence that each college and university enjoys. In Michigan every institution offering a baccalaureate degree is "constitutionally independent." There is no system of higher education combining separate institutions (although the University of Michigan has branch campuses at Dearborn and Flint), and there is no overall coordinating body with power effectively to influence educational policy.

In addition, there is no public employee bargaining law permitting bargaining over salaries by state employees. The Michigan public employee bargaining law applies to lower political jurisdictions, and the employees of colleges and universities have been bargaining under the existing law because of a ruling that they are not state employees.

State employee salaries have been set for many years by the Civil Service Commission, which submits its recommendations directly to the state legislature. These recommendations go into effect unless the legislature rejects them by a two-thirds vote.

As a result there is no state-level agency that exercises any substantial control over higher education as a state activity, and there is no state-level executive agency, such as an office of collective bargaining or other centralized bureaucracy, to develop and implement a collective bargaining policy either for state employees as a whole or for the institutions of higher education separately or in combination.

The state, of course, finances the institutions, and the budgetary process is a source of potential control even though the institutions have been diligent in asserting their constitutional independence in the courts. For example, a recent suit in the state supreme court by the three research universities (Michigan, Michigan State, and Wayne State) involves the issue of the right of the several governing boards to expend the money appropriated by the legislature for their institutions at their discretion. Victories in suits of this sort are important, but as a practical matter the wishes of the legislature are difficult to circumvent in the long run.

The institutions enjoy some independence with regard to finances, because not only do the major universities have substantial endowments and sources of extramural funds, but all institutions have the authority to set their own tuition charges. In 1973–74 these ranged from $465 at Saginaw State to $696 at the University of Michigan per year.

The four-year institutions of higher education in Michigan can be grouped into three categories:

1. The research universities: Michigan, Michigan State, and Wayne

State. The Wayne State faculty are organized and are represented by the American Association of University Professors.
2. The regional universities: Central, Northern, Western, and Eastern Michigan Universities. All of these are organized by the AAUP, except Central, which has a faculty association affiliated with the state branch of the NEA. Oakland University, which is represented by the AAUP, and Michigan Technological University, which is unorganized, are similar institutions.
3. The state colleges: Ferris, Saginaw Valley, Grand Valley, and Lake Superior. Ferris and Saginaw are represented by the NEA, while the other two are not organized.

Eight of the 13 four-year institutions are organized, five by the AAUP and three by the NEA. Central Michigan and Oakland were among the first colleges in the nation to unionize; Wayne, Eastern, and the two state colleges came later, while Northern and Western are negotiating their first contracts.

Although some informal contacts among the administrations of the different institutions, and among the various unions occur, there is little coordination or discussion of negotiation issues or strategy. Little discussion with the executive branch or the legislature seems to take place either prior to or during negotiations (with some qualifications to be noted later).

Budgets are prepared by each institution separately and are submitted to the executive branch. In recent years the department of education has been requiring increasingly detailed and analytical budgets, but this is not related to collective bargaining developments and is part of a move toward program budgeting generally. The governor transmits his recommendations to the legislature, which then holds hearings on the individual institutions' budgets. The institutions appear at these hearings and lobby for appropriations in the usual manner. As a general rule the faculty organizations do not seem to have been active participants in this phase, so far, except for the Wayne State group. At each of the three stages of the budgetary process a salary increase figure is built into the budget, at least implicitly. The increases proposed for state employees have been an important reference point at the executive and the legislative stage.

The collective bargaining negotiations go forward at the same time as the final stages of the budgetary process. In general, the increases granted to the faculty in negotiations have exceeded the amounts budgeted for salary increases by the legislature. Prior to faculty unionization, faculty salary increases had also occasionally exceeded the amounts provided by the state for this purpose in the general institutional budgets.

The internal budgetary adjustments necessary to meet these obligations have frequently required the administrations to shift money from other areas. To date the character of these transfers has not been challenged by the executive or the legislative branch.

Settlements for the institutions that have been bargaining longest have been in the 7–9 percent range over the years. The size of the increases has been questioned in annual legislative hearings and some criticism of them has been voiced by members. Some administrators believe that, unless the increases resulting from negotiations are soon brought more into line with those provided state employees, repercussions in the legislature are likely. In the absence of some sort of crisis, however, it is difficult to see how the legislature could make a control measure effective.

One method by which the legislature might intrude into decision-making would be to specify an amount to be expended for a specific program while cutting or holding the line on total budget appropriations. Wayne State might provide an example in the current situation. Wayne was anticipating an overall budget appropriation in July 1975 that would leave them with a deficit of $6 million for 1975–76. At the same time the legislature had provided an increase of almost $2 million for a medical program. The university's position was that it could shift the medical allocation at its own discretion, but spokesmen made it clear it would not do so.

The Michigan institutions are accustomed to handling their own lobbying in legislative committee proceedings, and the addition of faculty bargaining to the mixture has not changed the situation dramatically. There has been some increase in faculty lobbying through the unions and considerable criticism of the universities' settlements by the legislature, as noted earlier.

The relatively high faculty salary settlements in the past have squeezed the budgets of institutions, absorbing funds formerly available for other purposes and, some think, resulting in tuition increases. Tuitions, however, have been going up in all institutions, with or without bargaining. The institutions appear to believe that current poor conditions in the higher education labor market will permit them to negotiate settlements that they will be able to fit more easily into their budgets. Oakland abandoned the practice of submitting salary disputes to final offer arbitration in the belief that they will be able to negotiate settlements that will be lower than an arbitrator would award. There seems to be agreement that the limits of the encroachment of faculty salaries on other budget allocations have been reached and confidence that the administrations' bargaining position is strong enough to keep future increases within the bounds set by legislative appropriations.

In my opinion, this confidence may well turn out to be misplaced. The state's provision for salary increases for other employees will also be reduced in the present circumstances, and the reduction in faculty salary increases from previous settlements will have to be even greater to bring them into line with state employee increases. The colleges' record in negotiations has not been impressive in the past, and with each institution standing alone, their resolve will continue to be put to the test.

Michigan has an unusually high level of union activity in politics, and the system of bargaining in higher education encourages its growth. Wayne State illustrates this situation most dramatically. The three research universities have elected governing boards adding a touch of electoral politics to the Wayne State picture. In addition, although the AAUP won the representation election over the AFT at Wayne, the margin was 17 votes, and the AAUP had difficulty in staffing the union's positions in the new bargaining system. As a result the union from the beginning has drawn many of its staff and its officers from former AFT officers and activists. The influence of the national office of the AAUP on negotiations seems to have been relatively smaller than that of the United Auto Workers. A former UAW official has served as a consultant to the Wayne AAUP since the first negotiation. National officers of the UAW have been involved in the negotiations at Wayne and have accompanied the Wayne president to Lansing to discuss the range of acceptable settlements with the governor. One participant from the administration commented that Wayne "had been dealing with the representative of our representatives." This has had its advantages, because the administration believes that the UAW has given the faculty union the confidence needed to accept settlements that involved compromises of the demands of internal factions.

The UAW does not seem to have immediate ambitions to represent faculty units, but clearly they are competitors for nonfaculty groups. They represent nonacademic employees in some of the colleges, and the administrative staff unit at Eastern Michigan has recently chosen the UAW as their representative. The Wayne State administrative staff unit is reported to be close to switching from independent status to affiliation with the UAW.

Because the Michigan institutions control their own negotiations to an unusual degree and finance their settlements out of a lump sum budget that each institution negotiates with the governor's office and lobbies through the legislature, the system seems vulnerable to union encroachment in both financial and other matters through combinations of collective bargaining and lobbying at various points in the whole process. The present recession may mark a turning point by strengthening the institutions vis-à-vis the faculty unions, but the record of negotiations to date makes one skeptical of the institutions' ability to control the size of the concessions.

The situation in each state has unique elements, but my interpretation of the Michigan experience leads me to conclude that the threat to institutional independence in decision making is likely to be greater in this context than it would be in a system like New York's, with its centralized bargaining arrangements and executive initiative in financing. The Michigan arrangements seem to be susceptible to the process that a Pennsylvania analyst has called the "that's your problem" syndrome. In this sequence, when a college takes a firm stand on a bargaining issue to the point of impasse, the union lobbies the governor's office or the legislature to pressure the college administration to make concessions. When the college responds to this type of pressure by asking how the concessions will be financed, it gets the reply, "that's your problem." Unfortunately, as further examples show, this may occur in arrangements like New York's as well.

Hawaii. Although Hawaii is the only state included in the survey that was not facing something of a budget crisis, faculty unionism has had a difficult time for years. The state has a unique public employee bargaining law that specifies bargaining units for the whole state, identifies the composition of the employer side, permits strikes except under severely restricted conditions, and mandates the agency shop for any unit choosing a bargaining representative.

The University of Hawaii is a single comprehensive system including seven community colleges, and four-year campuses at Hilo, Hawaii, and Manoa, Oahu. The Manoa campus dominates the system, with 1,600 of the 2,500 members of the bargaining unit. The law provided that the university faculty would constitute a single bargaining unit with the administrative, technical, and professional staff as another separate university-based unit. The original bargaining election was won by the AFT, which negotiated a controversial contract that was repudiated by the faculty. After much jockeying, representation rights were won in another election by a combination of the AAUP chapter and the NEA affiliate running as the University of Hawaii Professional Assembly. A second round of negotiations produced a contract that won acceptance.

The law specified that the employer side for the university unit would be made up of three representatives from the governor's office and two from the board of regents. The first negotiation was handled by a private negotiator on retainer, the second by the director of the newly established office of employer relations in the governor's office. The intention is that all negotiations will be handled by the director in the future and an attempt is being made to arrange for contracts in all units to have a common expiration date. This approach suggests that the state hopes to have a common or at least a closely coordinated bargaining policy for all units.

The regents were represented in the second negotiation by the chairman and the vice-chairman of the board. The chairman is a lawyer with much experience in labor matters and had the authority to make decisions for the board. A separate staff committee of five persons headed by the secretary of the board represented the various institutions of higher education in the system. This committee functioned virtually as a bargaining committee when some of the academic issues were under consideration.

The employer committee went into bargaining with a limit to cost increases set by the governor. It was not able to settle within that limit and got authorization from the governor to exceed it to reach a settlement. The governor introduced appropriation bills to finance bargaining settlements, combining the funds needed for several other units and for an increase for the executive office staff with the university's financing.

Collective bargaining by faculty at the university has been conducted during a period of generalized conflict among the legislature, the board of regents, the university administration, and the faculty. The senate has passed resolutions directed against the faculty (for example, the weakening of tenure) and imposed budget cuts. Both the university president and the Manoa chancellor resigned in 1974. The chancellor resigned after a direct conflict with the regent who is now the chairman of the board and who was the key regent on the bargaining committee. The former chancellor returned to faculty status and is now chairman of the faculty senate.

Of the seven states surveyed, Hawaii is the only one where there seems to be a serious possibility that faculty collective bargaining might be the vehicle for intervention by the state into administrative and academic decision-making, with a majority of the board of regents as allies. Some members of the board seem to prefer to deal with the union rather than the faculty senate and to welcome the transfer of responsibility for employee affairs from the senate to the union. Bargaining is preferred to collegiality and consensus as a method of making decisions. The first contract negotiated with the AFT showed evidence of an aggressive employer stance in regard to provisions on tenure and management rights. The second contract takes a generally more moderate stand, but continuing conflicts over the management's right to change working conditions have been predicted. The issues will be tenure, workload, sabbaticals, and the other usual topics of conflict.

The union and the senate have a good working relationship at Hawaii with substantial overlap in leadership. They have tried to develop an interesting formal agreement specifying the areas of responsibility of each organization, and plan on joint efforts in lobbying and dealing with the administration.

If Hawaii is the state in which collective bargaining may be the instrument through which change is implemented, it may also be a state in which the faculty ability to resist change is maximized by the existence of the union. In my opinion, the changes that seem to be favored by a majority of the regents (and to have the support of the political establishment) have been generated by forces independent of the introduction of bargaining by faculty. Substituting bargaining for collegiality may offer the state and the governing board an opportunity to facilitate change while simultaneously increasing the ability of faculty to resist if matters come to an impasse. Stating the situation in this way, of course, does not necessarily imply approval or disapproval of the potential changes, but it appears that traditional state-institutional-faculty relations will be under stress in Hawaii for the foreseeable future. Collective bargaining will provide one area in which the struggle is likely to occur.

Pennsylvania. In Pennsylvania collective bargaining in public higher education centers on the state college system made up of 14 separate institutions.[3] These are state-owned institutions with separate boards of trustees, a relatively new overall Board of State Colleges and University Directors (SCUD), administered under a department of education headed by a secretary of education. The colleges have more than 4,000 faculty and about 70,000 students. The system is a single bargaining unit represented by the Association of Pennsylvania State College and University Professors (APSCUP), a NEA affiliate. The colleges have been organized since 1971 and negotiated an initial three-year contract that provided very generous economic benefits.

Pennsylvania also has a number of "state-related" universities, of which two, Temple and Lincoln, are organized. Pennsylvania State University is not a state university in the usual sense, but it is also "state-related," as is the University of Pittsburgh. Pittsburgh recently voted against unionization, and an organizing campaign is under way at Penn State. State-related universities receive a lump sum allocation from the state amounting to varying proportions of their budgets, but except for an essentially nominal budget review by the department of education, they operate independently. This includes handling their own bargaining with the responsibility of financing

---

[3]The system actually is made up of 13 state colleges and Indiana University, but for simplicity I will avoid the use of the formal title, State Colleges and University.

their settlements on their own. At least for purposes of collective bargaining, the state-related institutions have been determined to be public institutions under the jurisdiction of the state public employee bargaining law, but the state has had minimal effect on their internal bargaining.

The state college system has been undergoing a fairly rapid series of changes in recent years, the net result of which has been a centralization of control over the constituent institutions by the secretary of education. Faculty collective bargaining has been one of the developments that has contributed to the centralization of control.

Pennsylvania has a bureau of labor relations responsible for bargaining, but actual negotiations for higher education have been handled by professionals on retainer. The bargaining team has included several central headquarters personnel and two representatives designated by the presidents of the colleges. A unique feature of the second contract negotiated in 1974 was the provision for regular statewide "meet and discuss" meetings, whose participants have the power to make changes in the contract during its term.

The approach of the department of education to collective bargaining is summed up in the comment that it can be viewed as "one more management tool to control the state colleges as a system." The union claims to have originally supported the establishment of separate bargaining units for the colleges, but it now prefers the single unit, and the relations between the union and the department of education appear to be unusually cooperative. The union has cultivated good relations with the organized students to minimize possible conflicts on such issues as tuition increases.

The department's belief that bargaining might be used as a management tool seems to mean that by bargaining with the union at the statewide level it is able to influence such subjects as personnel policies and teaching evaluation on the separate campuses directly without relying solely on managerial authority to implement changes through the usual chain of command. That the secretary is not averse to the direct exercise of authority, however, is illustrated by a widely reported incident that occurred in June. Facing a budget problem, the secretary decided to make a major reduction in personnel and directed each president to submit a list of persons to be "retrenched" by 5:00 Monday, June 30. One president announced that he could meet the monetary savings goal by other means and that therefore he did not intend to submit names. He was immediately notified that unless the names were submitted by June 30, "... it is the Governor's intention to remove you from the Office of President ... as of 9:00 a.m., Tuesday, July 1, 1975. ..." The names were submitted.

An aggressive secretary of education in Pennsylvania has shown signs of taking on some of the functions of a chancellor of a multi-institutional system of higher education. The systemwide bargaining unit has made collective bargaining a force assisting the process of centralization. The college presidents in the system have a formal association with an executive secretary and offices in Harrisburg. They are disturbed by the loss of influence on system affairs by them-selves and by the Board of State Colleges and University Directors. It is reported that SCUD recommended retrenchment of personnel in the past, but found that the department and the union had signed a memorandum of agreement guaranteeing no retrenchment as part of the first settlement. Other recommendations by SCUD have also been blocked by union-department agreement. On the other hand, one col-lege president reported that, as a result of the statewide meet and dis-cuss meetings, "bargaining has illuminated the thinking and height-ened the awareness of central administrators. ... It is now much less likely that faculty rights will be overridden by bureaucratic rules and regulations. ..."

In a sense Pennsylvania could be seen as a clear-cut example of a situation where collective bargaining has contributed to an encroach-ment of a state agency on institutional independence. In my opinion it is more accurate to see these developments as part of an evolution from a system of independent institutions to an integrated system of higher education. The secretary of education seems to be acting less as an agent of the governor or the legislature than as an embryonic chan-cellor of a new system of higher education. This interpretation is sup-ported by the existence of a proposal for converting the state colleges to the "Pennsylvania Commonwealth University" directly under the governor and outside the control of the department of education. This proposal is reported to be supported by all parties, the union, the department, and the association of presidents.

Turning to the financing of contracts, the Pennsylvania approach resembles that of New York State. The governor has followed a system of submitting separate legislation to finance the bargaining settlements. Pennsylvania's experience demonstrates that this approach is not foolproof from either the institution's or the union's point of view. The appropriation bill has typically been submitted for less than the amount needed to finance the settlement, other things remaining equal, and the institutions have had to finance the nonfunded portion from other sources. The union has charged that this tactic is illegal in that the governor is required to request funding to meet costs, but the governor's official position is that, as long as the pay rates called for in the contract are met, the supplementary appropriation can be set on the assumption that other cost-saving changes are to be made. In other words, in setting the amount needed to fund the contracts, the governor can assume that some part will come from savings in other areas of the institutions' budgets.

This suggests how difficult it is to devise structural or procedural mechanisms that cannot be circumvented by an ingenious and determined state administration operating under financial pressure.

Massachusetts. Until 1975 Massachusetts law did not permit bargaining on economic issues by public employees; faculty unions are therefore engaged in a drawn-out first attempt at negotiating these issues, and the parties have been feeling their way.

Massachusetts has a system of community colleges originally designated as separate bargaining units but recently consolidated into a single unit represented by the NEA affiliate. It has a system of ten state colleges (including a maritime college), seven of which were organized as of mid-1975. Four have NEA representatives, while three have AFT unions. The colleges are separate bargaining units, although they all bargain with a single central administration.

Massachusetts also has two state universities, the University of Massachusetts and Southeastern Massachusetts University; the latter's faculty has been represented by the AFT since 1969–70. A third university, Lowell University, has just been established by combining Lowell State College and the Lowell Institute of Technology. The two component institutions were both organized, one by the NEA and one by the AFT. The representation of the new institution has not been settled. In fact, every public institution of higher education in Massachusetts either is organized or is expected to hold a bargaining election in the near future.

At the moment the Massachusetts bargaining structure most closely resembles the Michigan model. There is no central office of employee relations. Each of the five segments of higher education (the community colleges, the state colleges, and the three universities) has its own board of trustees that functions as the employer and is responsible for negotiations.

Each segment submits its budget for review by an executive office overseeing education. Executive review has not been important in the past, but its role is growing. As in Michigan, there is no formal mechanism for coordinating negotiations in higher education, but unlike Michigan, Massachusetts has separate legislative action for financing the cost items that appear in the several contracts. As it is presently envisaged, the governor plays little role in the financing process, the parties submitting their requests for funding directly to the appropriate legislative committee. Although some contracts had been negotiated as early as the beginning of 1975, the legislature has been clearly reluctant to take final action until the salary situation has been clarified in the state as a whole. The parties to bargaining were finding settlements reached after intensive bargaining held up at the legislative stage.

The reason for this tentative description is not only that this has been the first time around for the bargaining process, but also that Massachusetts has been in serious financial straits. The governor has been trying to hold the line on salaries for all employees. It is of interest that, in contrast to Rhode Island, both parties seem to agree that an attempt to enforce a salary freeze by the state would not preclude the parties from negotiating increases. It would simply mean that they were bargaining over shares of the existing budget totals.

As noted in other sections of this report, the well-publicized participation of students in bargaining in some of the state colleges ended when salaries became a bargainable issue. The state colleges, however, are experimenting with another procedure of considerable interest. In the units represented by the AFT, the administration and the union have organized a two-tier bargaining system. A joint bargaining team negotiates on economic issues while noneconomic issues are discussed by other teams at the campus level. There is some coordination through overlapping membership among the negotiators at each level. The historic separation of economic and noneconomic issues in Massachusetts may make this pattern more workable than in some other states, and it appears to be a desirable arrangement to adapt bargaining to the needs of the local campuses.

Now that economic issues are bargainable in Massachusetts, the separate bargaining units for the several state college campuses are likely to be challenged and perhaps replaced by a single unit. It seems unrealistic to believe that significant differences in economic settlements will be tolerated among the several institutions, particularly when all contracts are negotiated by a single administrative office. Although separate election petitions have been filed for the unorganized campuses, pressure will almost certainly develop for the formation of a single bargaining unit in the state college system. It is less certain but also probable that the governor's role in the process will also be enlarged in the future. Both of these developments would be likely to increase centralization in Massachusetts higher education.

New Jersey. Public higher education in New Jersey is highly organized, with most interest centering on the New Jersey State College System and Rutgers University. Other senior public institutions are New Jersey Institute of Technology and the College of Medicine and Dentistry.

Rutgers was one of the first universities to organize and is one of the few single-campus institutions with a large graduate program and a strong research orientation that has a faculty union. Along with St. John's University, it is the showcase AAUP unit in the sense that the bargaining relationship comes closest to following the pattern favored by the national AAUP. This includes supporting the role of the faculty senate, incorporating AAUP policy into contract language, and emphasizing the inclusion of procedures for settling conflicts into the contract rather than attempting to specify solutions by writing them into the contract language.

Rutgers had a large, active AAUP chapter when the passage of public employee bargaining legislation raised the prospect of organization. At about the same time, changes in the organization of higher education, particularly the creation of the office of chancellor at the state level, indicated a move to establish central control over all of public higher education. In an attempt to preserve its separate status and avoid being swept into a statewide bargaining unit, the Rutgers AAUP launched a campaign to secure representation rights. The campaign was successful without the necessity of an election, which is one reason why the Rutgers relationship has been relatively harmonious.

The strategy has worked rather well so far. Rutgers bargains and signs its own contract with the union, with contact being maintained between the negotiating team and the Office of Employee Relations in Trenton. In one contract, the state balked at one of the provisions that had been negotiated and the contract was placed into effect while talks continued on the disputed point. Rutgers' fear that the chancellor would try to extend control over their operations has to some extent been justified, but it has not been related to the collective bargaining process. In the past the Rutgers president has been one of the few administrators to speak favorably of faculty bargaining. This attitude seems to be changing. The level of conflict is rising, exacerbated by a budget crisis and the prospect of retrenchment of faculty. One of the causes of friction has been the addition of about 800 employed graduate students to the 1700 person faculty bargaining unit at administration initiative. Student fringe benefits became a major issue in negotiations and some resentment of the situation appeared among groups of faculty in the union.

In the previous, more salubrious financial climate, Rutgers was able to include an anticipated salary increase in its current-year budget, enter into negotiations, and come out with a settlement within the budgeted amount. In general, the settlements were approximately the same as the increases granted other state employees. Recent negotiations have been conducted in the context of a budget squeeze and the results will have to be accommodated within a very tight budget total established by the state.

The state college system includes eight state colleges that bargain as a single unit. The original elections were won by the state NEA affiliate, the New Jersey Education Association. The AFT challenged the representation status of the NEA at the end of the first contract and won over them by a single vote. Negotiations broke down in 1974, and the AFT conducted the first systemwide strike in a four-year institution.

In contrast to Rutgers, state college bargaining is conducted by the governor's Office of Employee Relations. An unusual feature is that the Director of Employee Relations assigns one of his staff full time to the Office of the Chancellor to serve as the labor relations officer for the chancellor. This representative is characterized as a joint employee and serves as liaison between the two departments for all higher education bargaining, with actual bargaining handled by the director of the OER or his deputy. The team has included a minority of representatives from the colleges, but there are plans to develop a more elaborate system of advisory committees for future negotiations to meet criticism that present procedures do not provide enough participation by the colleges.

The strike in the fall of 1974 precipitated a bitter conflict between the chancellor and the governor's office, which might seem to indicate that an encroachment on institutional independence was involved. The two-week strike was essentially lost by the union and the question arose as to whether the striking faculty would be able to make up the time and pay lost during the walk-out. The new governor had been elected with strong labor support, and his office intervened to negotiate an arrangement whereby it would be possible for a faculty member to make up his lost pay if additional duties were available to be performed. The chancellor objected to this arrangement and was also critical of the failure of the governor to secure an injunction against the strike.

Perhaps in part because of the strike, students have been more active in New Jersey than in other states, but this does not seem to have produced significant results on the bargaining process.

The governor's action hardly seems to amount to an incursion into institutional decision making in any substantive way. The lesson would seem to be that a faculty strike in a state institution of higher education is likely to lead to intervention by the executive or the legislature if it continues for any length of time. As long as the institution's budget comes from the state, this is likely to be true whatever the formal bargaining structure.

Rhode Island. Public higher education in Rhode Island consists of three institutions, all unionized. The University of Rhode Island is organized by the AAUP, Rhode Island College by the AFT, and

Rhode Island Junior College by the NEA. A single board of trustees controls all levels of higher education and functions as the employer, conducting all negotiations. Although the board is responsible for the negotiating, the responsible staff member meets regularly with the governor to report and to receive guidance.

Each institution prepares its own budget and submits it to the board of regents, which reviews them and makes recommendations to the governor. In the past the institutions have included the proposed salary increases for the coming year in their budgets. The most interesting development in Rhode Island is that in 1975 the legislature officially took the stand that no increases in salaries or changes in fringe benefits requiring additional funding would be made prior to July 1, 1976. The regents have taken the position that this precludes negotiating an increase. The unions argue that an increase can be financed out of the existing budget appropriations consistent with the language of the legislature's action. The AAUP has charged that the regents' position amounts to a refusal to bargain in good faith.

This illustrates a general problem under public employee bargaining that is likely to be common in states with budget crises. In both Rhode Island and Massachusetts the governors had taken the stand that no increases would be provided state employees in 1975. When the governor is not the employer (that is, not in direct control of negotiations), the unions take the position that the governor or the legislature is doing no more than announcing that no appropriations will be specifically earmarked to fund wage increases. Under some budgetary procedures, this may not preclude agencies, including universities, from granting pay increases financed by shifting funds around in the general budget or from other funds under their control. In Michigan an internal "battle of the budget" has been waged when the institutions have given larger increases than the legislature provided. In Massachusetts and Rhode Island the governors tried to hold salary-increase funds to zero, but the principle is the same in all three states.

SUMMARY

In four of the seven states (New York, New Jersey, Pennsylvania, and Hawaii) an agency of the executive office functions as the employer and conducts negotiations. In all except New Jersey the general institutional budget for the current year has been handled separately from the funding of the negotiated settlements. In Michigan, Massachusetts, and CUNY in New York, the governing boards of the separate institutions or systems are the employers and negotiate the contracts. In Rhode Island the single overall governing board negotiates for all public institutions. In all of these latter instances the financing of the negotiated settlements is the responsibility of the institutions as part of the general budgetary process.

While in both patterns the institutions lobby in the legislature, the second pattern puts more pressure on the institutions both in dealing with their unions and in ensuring favorable treatment from the legislature. A preference for one system over the other depends on whether the threat of encroachment on institutional independence from the executive office is greater or less than the threat from the unions *(not just the faculty unions)* and the legislature. In Hawaii, for example, the threat of intervention by the state seems to be greater than the threat from the unions.

In my opinion, the trend in the states will be toward identifying the chief executive as the employer in order to bring the coordination of pay policy for state employees into a single office under the control of the governor. Where the institutions remain as the employer of record, and are therefore the negotiators, close coordination between the governor's office and the bargainers in the Rhode Island pattern will probably develop, thereby reducing the differences between the two approaches.

Students' Relation to Faculty Bargaining[4]

Students have shown an active concern with the effect of faculty bargaining on their interests with most of the attention focused on two areas:

1. In those institutions whose students feel that they have achieved a position of influence in the traditional governance structures, the introduction of bargaining is seen as a transfer of power to a new structure in which they have no role.
2. In addition to believing that they will be excluded from participating in the new decision-making process, organized students feel

[4]In the following sections the reports by states will not be given separately.

that the decisions made will raise costs, affect personnel policies, program decisions, educational practices, and other matters.

In other words, students are interested in the effect of bargaining on their participation in governance and in the potential detrimental results of bargaining on their interests. The usual student response is to try to protect their newly won role in traditional structures and at the same time to try to achieve participation in the bargaining arrangements.

There is very little experience with direct student participation in bargaining. The much publicized situation in the Massachusetts state college system has been greatly exaggerated in its extent and significance. Of the ten institutions (including the maritime academy) only seven were unionized. No student participation has occurred in the colleges represented by the AFT. Participation in the others varied and was at the invitation of the NEA locals and the state college administration. During the period of student participation salaries and other economic items were excluded from bargaining by law. Most of the resulting contracts dealt with governance issues, including student participation in committees. Opinions as to the results are mixed, but I believe the consensus is that student participation was passive and not consequential. With the introduction of bargaining on economic issues, students have been excluded altogether by agreement of the parties.

At the City Colleges of Chicago students have on occasion been admitted as observers. Students in Chicago and in other community colleges have taken actions, such as securing injunctions, outside the framework of negotiations to deal with the results of impasses.

In recent months Oregon and Montana have passed legislation that permits student participation in faculty negotiations. In Montana the first contracts have been negotiated. Preliminary reports are that in one institution little or no participation occurred, in another the student representative carried out discussions with the parties, while in the third the students have been interested but relatively passive.

Fragmentary evidence suggests that, with regard to governance, the first area of concern identified above, bargaining may well turn out to have increased student participation. No systematic evidence is available, but in many contracts students are given specific rights with respect to such issues as committee membership and the evaluation of teaching that they had not had before. Bargaining seems to have provided the occasion for introducing questions of student participation, and at least some of the students' desires seem to have been accommodated. The parties seem to have been willing to allow this at least partly as a way of avoiding other types of student participation. Faced with demands by students for inclusion in negotiations, both faculty and administrations may have been more receptive to proposals for other alternative forms of participation, such as membership on senate committees.

It should be noted that this appears to parallel the way in which faculty bargaining has affected faculty senates. In theory faculty unionism would be expected to take over the representation function, ousting the senates from the decision-making process. In fact, up to this time, there appears to be a consensus that the senate system has been strengthened by the advent of faculty unionism in more instances than it has been weakened.

Incidentally, the question of whether increased student participation in governance has improved the educational process has seldom been addressed. It is not obvious why organized faculty action is generally assumed to pose a threat and organized student action to promise benefits to educational objectives.

Turning to the effect of bargaining on student costs, faculty union contracts often provide that, if a conflict exists between an administrative policy and the contract, the contract rules. This possibility is the source of the student interest in the interaction of governance and unionism. Traditional academic governance practices seem not to have been affected by unionism to the degree expected, largely because bargaining has so far tended to be limited to salaries and personnel matters.

Even if this assessment is accepted, the problem of financing the direct and indirect costs of concessions in times of financial stringency may require adjustments in a wide range of areas of operation, many of them impinging on student interests. Needless to say, cost increases stem from many sources other than faculty unionism, but the large fraction of total costs accounted for by faculty salaries makes this item particularly important.

Most professionals in industrial relations, neutrals and participants alike, are opposed to third party intervention into collective bargaining negotiations. In fact, it is regarded as a mark of maturity and procedural sophistication that private sector bargaining has increasingly been conducted out of public view. One indication of the remarkable degree to which privacy is respected in private bargaining is the newspapers' practice of reporting the fact that negotiators have reached agreement, but withholding the terms of the settlement until they have been communicated to union membership. Only after the membership have voted to accept or reject the agreement are the terms announced by the press. (This may represent the only example of journalistic restraint still regularly practiced in a world of "investigative reporting.")

Industrial relations specialists regard industrial peace as a fragile balance of political and economic pressures difficult to achieve and in constant danger of disintegration. Negotiations often involve a tedious and complex series of compromises and concessions in which the interests of many opposing groups are at stake. On both the union and the administrative side, the results of negotiations invariably leave a wide range of interests unsatisfied compared with the aspirations or expectations entertained by some group at some point in the proceedings. As the specialists see it, negotiations are another example of a need to strike a balance between representative effectiveness and participative democracy. The experts see negotiation as a method of reaching workable decisions, not as a form of group therapy or political theater. The current practices in major private sector bargaining probably represent too closed a system, but multilateral negotiations or bargaining in the "sunshine" may be unworkable in terms of administrative feasibility and institutional stability.

From the administration's and the public's point of view, multilateral bargaining poses the problem of the scope of bargaining in an even more acute form than that already existing. When the Wayne State administration decided to try to meet its $6 million deficit for 1975–76 by a three-pronged approach of raising tuition, cutting operating budgets, and negotiating a reduction in the pay increase scheduled for that year, it treated the first two decisions as managerial prerogatives. Of course, it is unlikely that a bargaining situation in which negotiations are limited to faculty would not be open to pressures to widen the scope of bargaining to include such items as tuition or budget allocations in other areas. In the course of negotiations at Wayne State, the administration and the faculty union agreed to finance jointly a study of university operations by a management consulting firm. In this context it would seem likely that the range of university decisions that would be brought into question could be very broad indeed. Nevertheless, there are precedents for dividing issues into mandatory and permissive subjects for bargaining both in the private sector and in the public sector.

The possibilities of limiting the scope of bargaining to a specific range of issues in any single negotiation in the public sector are not good. Particularly during budget stringency, public bargaining has tended to expand to cover all the elements in the budget. Bargaining with different occupational and interest groups separately could, at least in theory, permit the parties to limit the subjects included in each negotiation to those most relevant to the group engaged in bargaining. The inclusion of multiple groups in single negotiations will broaden the scope of bargaining to encompass all the topics of concern to each separately. It may be that this sort of mass negotiation over budgetary allocations will turn out to be necessary in higher education bargaining, but if so, the resulting process will be quite different from private sector bargaining. The participants may find the much-maligned "industrial model" of unexpected utility and increasingly attractive.

The point may be illustrated by another example with some unexpected implications. At CUNY the board of higher education instituted a system of student evaluation of faculty at least in part at the instigation of the organized students. The faculty union filed an unfair labor practice charge, arguing that the board had a duty to bargain with it about the evaluation procedures. The New York Public Employment Relations Board (PERB) ruled that the evaluation system was not a mandatory subject of bargaining. The student organization regarded this as an important victory.

The student group earlier had tried unsuccessfully to be included in the negotiations, and this suggests some interesting questions. If the students had been party to the faculty negotiations, could the board have successfully maintained that the evaluation system was not a bargainable issue? If the faculty had demanded that the board bargain with them in bilateral negotiations about the amount of money to be made available for student aid, would this have been a mandatory subject of bargaining? If not, would the level of student aid have been a mandatory subject of bargaining if the students were part of a multilateral bargaining process?

The administrations also might prefer to deal separately with organized students on questions of student financial aid and with organized faculty on questions of faculty salaries. Do the parties really want to deal in joint session with the whole range of problems? Or does student participation in faculty bargaining mean that students can influence the terms of faculty-administration settlements, but that such student issues as financial aid will be nonnegotiable?

Although the budgetary process in public universities and colleges is hardly isolated from interest group pressure now, trying to settle all allocation questions in a version of an open bargaining forum operating under law and court review is not likely to improve matters.

Academic bargaining is most likely to work if the process is viewed as a series of bilateral negotiations with the administration participating in each as the representative of the general interest. Almost any system, including multilateral bargaining, will work if there are no serious conflicts of interest. Where such conflicts exist, bilateral bargaining obviously will not work perfectly, but is more likely to produce workable solutions than multilateralism. Students, for example, might very well do better dealing separately with the administration and the faculty, than they would as participants in a formally multilateral bargaining system. In fact, students on balance appear to be doing quite well in protecting their interests with virtually no formal participation in the current state of higher education bargaining.

The recognition of the fact that students are likely to develop an informal variety of bilateral negotiations with administrations (and possibly faculty) through student governments or other organizations raises the question of whether students should be granted the legal right to organize and bargain collectively. Massachusetts is considering the adoption of such a policy.

In my opinion, giving organized students anything like the right to organize and to demand "bargaining in good faith" in the pattern established in American industrial relations would be a serious mistake. It would encourage the development of a professional "student" leadership and the politicization of student relations in the European or possibly the South American model. Given the demonstrated effectiveness of the present lobbying activities of organized students, the electoral power of concentrated student communities with the lowered voting age and casual voting registration procedures, and the power provided students by the competition of institutions, of schools and departments, and of faculty members for students, the extension of a bargaining system designed for very different circumstances to the student population does not seem to serve a useful purpose. Informal representation and even negotiation are probably inevitable and, considered as consultation, often desirable, but in the United States "collective bargaining in good faith" implies a system of legal apparatus and procedures that should not be introduced into student relations.

Bargaining and Multi-Institutional Systems

The introduction of faculty bargaining into higher education occurred at a time when a clear-cut move to greater centralization of decision-making was already well under way. Centralization has taken several forms, including integrating separate campuses into systems of institutions, strengthening central administration control in existing loosely knit systems, merging previously independent systems into larger, more comprehensive systems, and establishing superboards or councils to coordinate higher education in a state as a whole. All but the last pattern of centralization are relevant to this discussion, since the great majority of faculty covered by collective bargaining are to be found in the more or less integrated systems of CUNY, SUNY, Hawaii, Rhode Island, Florida, and the Pennsylvania, New Jersey, Minnesota, and Massachusetts state colleges.

Collective bargaining is a powerful reinforcement of the existing tendencies toward centralization. Of the multi-institutional systems noted above, all except the Massachusetts state colleges have been declared to be single bargaining units for faculty organization. (With the introduction of bargaining about salaries, it is predicted that the Massachusetts units will be amalgamated. The system already has systemwide units of nonacademic employees.) New Jersey originally had separate units for each state college campus, but they have been consolidated.

Even without a conscious policy of encouraging centralization, system administration finds itself forced to centralize and standardize faculty personnel policy to a greater degree than formerly. In dealing with a single union, an administration that has not standardized policy and controlled its implementation will find itself pressured to "level up" every concession made on any of its campuses. Perhaps more important, the negotiation process forces previously informal practices to be made explicit and brings them into the open so that they become subjects of bargaining, and cross-campus comparison. In addition to personnel policies a great deal more budget information is brought into the public domain under bargaining, and pressures toward uniform treatment are increased. In multi-institutional systems these forces fuel the process of centralization in the system-wide office even when that office is not aggressively seeking to expand its control.

In several of the systems that have organized, a major expansion of central control over the separate campuses was already under way, often at the initiative of the governor or the legislature. (New Jersey provides an example.) In these cases the offices of the secretary of education or the chancellor have sometimes seen bargaining as a "management tool" that permits a central office to influence developments on individual campuses in a direct way. A policy on promotion, salary administration, retrenchment, discipline, or teaching evaluation can be negotiated into the collective bargaining contract, which then becomes applicable immediately and uniformly throughout the system. The problems that arise in implementing these provisions are brought to the top administrative level for settlement by the operation of the grievance procedure.

In these latter instances, it appears that collective bargaining can provide state officials in the executive and the legislative branch with a way to increase their influence on academic policy insofar as they influence the negotiators on the administrative side either directly or indirectly.

As some campus presidents have pointed out, there are sometimes advantages in having the union independently bring problems to the attention of central administration to reinforce local administration's own positions on the same issues. Coalitions of faculty union leadership and college administrators may be increasingly common. In general, however, the heads of the several campuses of multi-institutional systems are the sources of the strongest criticisms of the operation of collective bargaining in higher education. They typically feel that they do not have enough influence in the negotiation process itself, that the resulting contracts do not recognize the existence of and the desirability of local diversity, and that their attempts to administer the contracts so as to try to minimize these problems are undercut by the actions of higher authority, usually as expressed through decisions on appeals in the grievance procedure.

Experience in the private sector with the analogous problem of multiplant companies suggests that the union is more likely than plant management to stress the need for "local supplements" to deal with local issues. Some faculty union locals complain about centralization brought about by bargaining, but the local administrations in higher education seem to be much more concerned with the problem.

Although the mechanisms for participation vary, all of the negotiators for the multi-institutional systems try to provide for input from the separate campuses. The realities of the bargaining process make it hard to provide all of the interested groups with comprehensive and continuous representation of their views; some groups will always find that their interests have been sacrificed or compromised in the final settlement.

The best that can be hoped for in the circumstances is that the parties attempt to separate those issues on which systemwide uniformity is necessary from those for which local variation is important and possible and to encourage something like the two-tier negotiation being tried in the AFT units of the Massachusetts state colleges. Where the separate institutions are similar in their educational function, the degree of diversity needed to maintain functional efficiency is probably exaggerated by the parties. Even in heterogeneous systems, the differences that have to be recognized and dealt with in the contracts may not be as great as traditionally believed. At SUNY the faculty at the university centers, after years of generalized anxiety over the alleged homogenization of policy, have been given the opportunity to identify those specific areas where differentiation is essential. According to reports, finding such areas has not been an easy task.

SUNY-Buffalo, however, has consistently retained some special features of its previous academic system. It is desirable that the central administrations of both the union and the system lean over backward to preserve institutional diversity in policy and the burden of proof that standardization is necessary should be on the central offices.

Particularly in heterogeneous systems including different types of institutions, the central administration in the long run probably has as great a stake in preserving differentials as any of the separate campuses. Uniformity may have the virtue of administrative simplicity, but it may be detrimental in both its cost and its educational consequences. The danger is that practices affecting costs may be leveled up and those affecting performance may be leveled down.

Bargaining Units and Internal Administration

Three different problems can be grouped under this heading: (1) the problem of dealing with unions of employed students; (2) the problem of organized "middle management" groups, and (3) the problem of the agency shop.

A great deal of discussion of issues raised by the possible heterogeneity of the "faculty" bargaining unit has been carried on, particularly in large institutions with substantial numbers of academic and support professionals such as librarians and full-time researchers. A newer version of the same problem has appeared as graduate students working as research and teaching assistants show signs of organizing. If the faculties of institutions with sizable numbers of such student employees organize, the question arises as to whether separate bargaining units ought to be established or whether the student and faculty organizations ought to be combined.

At CUNY graduate students have been in the unit since the beginning and they do not seem to have created any special problems (possibly because other problems have loomed larger). At Rutgers about 800 graduate students were included in the faculty unit of some 1,700 persons by agreement after organization occurred and this has created difficulties. The student issue is being considered at SUNY although it is not a current problem. Student unions have been recognized and have negotiated their own contracts at Wisconsin and Michigan, where faculty are not unionized. Although the issue is not likely to be serious or even to exist at most unionized institutions, in institutions with large graduate programs it may become important.

As a general principle, graduate students ought not to be included in faculty units. In addition to the problems of supervisor-employee relations that exist between faculty and student assistants, the agenda of concerns of a union reflects the interests of self-selected activist groups of members. Organized students may exert a disproportionate influence on the selection of the topics that are considered at the negotiating table. Because of the low degree of interest in participation in collective bargaining by large sections of professionally oriented established faculty, relatively small organized segments of the membership of the bargaining units, particularly in large institutions, determine the issues that will get most attention.

This is not to say that the interests of separate occupational groups should not be represented in the bargaining structure. In fact, it will be impossible to prevent such representation. It is easier to amalgamate or federate bargaining structures, however, if true community of interests turns out to exist than it is to break up conglomerate units once they are established. Administrations should restrain their desire to minimize the number of units recognized for bargaining.

The problem of the increasing tendency for "middle management" employees to organize is a related but different issue. In many institutions nonteaching staff members who do not exercise supervisory or policy functions are part of the faculty units. In others they have been excluded. In the latter instances, these groups have tended to unionize and bargain on their own as at Wayne State, Eastern Michigan, Hawaii, and Rhode Island College. This development raises many of the same issues as those noted in the discussion of organized students and most of the same considerations apply.

A new form of the problem is potentially more troublesome. A more critical set of administrators—such as associate and assistant deans, directors and functional department managers—are showing signs of restiveness. They often have some of the same grievances as other professional groups and would like to achieve some of the same benefits as their unionized colleagues. More important, as relatively highly paid staff, they are often chosen to furnish examples of salary restraint by an administration trying to provide models of reasonable behavior to unionized groups. At least partly as a result, at some institutions the proportion of "management" not represented by unions is shrinking as administrators decide to form their own unions. Administrators need to give more attention to defining managerial roles and devising policies to encourage identification of the incumbents with "management" and to minimize the possibility that the university will consist of layers of organized employees with a small cadre of top administrators left as official management.

As an example of the process noted above, in 1976 a bargaining unit of administrative employees of the Massachusetts state college system was established that included all administrative staff except the central office staff, the presidents, and the deans. Bargaining rights were won by the National Association of Government Employees (NAGE), which defeated the state AFT and NEA affiliates and the Teamsters Union. Some of these managerial units are represented by independent staff associations, some have chosen one of the teachers' units to represent them, and some have chosen unions such as NAGE (a union whose primary base is among federal employees) or the UAW.

The agency shop is becoming a live issue in more states as public employee bargaining expands.

The bargaining laws of Hawaii and Rhode Island provide that the agency shop is automatically placed in force when a bargaining agent is chosen. Other states, such as New York, prohibit the use of the agency shop, while a growing number, such as Massachusetts and Michigan, permit the parties to negotiate the issue. The trend is toward permitting the parties to agree on the practice, but not to mandate it in legislation.

From the union point of view, the mandating of the agency shop in legislation is the ideal solution to the problem of the willingness of faculty to vote for unionization while remaining reluctant to join and pay dues. It provides the union with financial security while relieving it of the onus of taking the unpopular action of compelling contributions. (The negotiation of an agency shop at Central Michigan after several years when voluntary membership remained at a relatively low level was a major factor in sparking a move to decertify the union.) Supporting the mandatory agency shop has some practical advantages for employers because it provides financial security for the union, but American employers in general have been reluctant to support this approach and universities as employers have more reason than most to oppose it because it raises questions about tenure and academic freedom.

The typically low proportion of voluntary membership in union bargaining units (50 percent membership among eligible faculty is a common situation) presents the unions with a dilemma. The members supporting the union resent the large percentage of "free riders," but an attempt to force the others into contributing may threaten the status of the union as a representative in a decertification or challenge election. The problem is complicated by the incompatibility of traditional tenure and the compulsory payment of fees on pain of termination. A court case involving members of the Ferris State College faculty, where the contract requires compulsory membership, is currently pending.

A unique approach to dealing with this problem has been used at Central Michigan and Youngstown State. The contracts there provided for the payment of agency shop service fees, but the payment is not made a condition of employment to be enforced by the employer. Instead the union is expected to collect the fee from a reluctant faculty member through a civil suit. It is not possible to predict whether this approach will withstand the legal challenges that appear to be inevitable.

The traditional American approach to the problem of compulsory membership in most industries has been for employers to wait for the union to achieve high levels (75 percent or more) of voluntary membership before granting the union or agency shop. In particular instances, an administration or union might be wise to institutionalize the union by negotiating the agency shop at a low level of voluntary membership, but in the general case the traditional approach of holding off until a substantial majority has joined voluntarily has merit and should be followed. So far, experience in higher education suggests that faculty unions will be reluctant to push for compulsory membership in negotiations until they have achieved relatively high levels of voluntary membership.

Concluding Remarks

In considering the main question of the influence that faculty collective bargaining has had on state-institution relations, two general types of situations can be identified:

Those institutions or institutional systems with relatively well-established internal functional structures and stable external relations with the executive branch in their states have experienced some changes, but these have not had major consequences for academic affairs. This appears to be true whether the governor's office or the institutions handle the actual bargaining with the unions. Examples of this type are SUNY in New York, Rutgers in New Jersey, Temple University in Pennsylvania, and the Massachusetts and the Michigan colleges and universities. These institutions still control their own academic destinies within the limits of their budgets and their problems with the state are primarily budgetary. In this respect they do not differ much from their nonunionized brethren in public higher education as far as external relations are concerned.

In some cases there seems to be an increase in the extent to which institutions in this category have had their salary and personnel policies tied to those for other public employees. In the multi-institutional systems, the institutional and union leadership on the campuses see power displaced to the central administration and occasionally to a limited extent, to the executive branch of state government.

The other major type of situation is that of the "emerging" institution or, more likely, systems of institutions. The structure of internal institutional relations, and usually of state-institution relations as well, has little historical tradition on which to rely in handling their problems. The faculty unions, the executive offices of employee relations, the governor and the legislature, the higher education bureaucracy, and the campus executives are to some extent maneuvering for position in an evolving situation without the benefit of experience. The way in which control over higher education is going to be distributed is in question in a direct and obvious way. The new collective bargaining system is one of the vehicles the parties may use to influence the outcome of the competition. To date, the central administrations have probably gained most from the introduction of bargaining, by acquiring some influence over affairs on the campuses while yielding little to the executive or the legislature. This trend is likely to continue, in part because the systemwide bargaining units make the central administrations of both the universities and the faculty unions the natural locus of most decision making, at least on issues outside the area of educational policy.

Part Three

Legislative Issues in Faculty Collective Bargaining

David E. Feller

Professor of Law
University of California, Berkeley

Matthew W. Finkin

Professor of Law
Southern Methodist University

1

An Overview

The focus of this study is upon legislation governing collective bargaining for faculty in institutions of higher education. Our objectives are to identify the legislative issues which are peculiar to higher education, to examine the way in which those issues have been dealt with in existing legislation, and to recommend what seem to the authors to be the most desirable method of dealing with them.*

Essentially two kinds of legislation deal with faculty collective bargaining in higher education. The first concerns the private sector. There the applicable statute, at least for institutions having a certain minimum impact upon interstate commerce, is the National Labor Relations Act (NLRA). That Act has no special provisions to deal with the peculiar characteristics of faculty bargaining and until 1970 it was not applied to institutions of higher education at all.[1] Since that date the National Labor Relations Board (NLRB) has struggled with varying success to fit to faculty collective bargaining statutory provisions designed to deal with the far different employment relationships in American industry.[2] Although this has created prob-

---

*Because Matthew W. Finkin also serves as General Counsel to the American Association of University Professors, it is of special importance to note that the views expressed are entirely the authors'.

[1] Cornell University, 183 NLRB 329 (1970).

[2] See generally M. W. Finkin, "The NLRB in Higher Education," 5 *U. Tol. L. Rev.* 608 (1974) [hereinafter Finkin] and the sources cited therein. See also D. Pollitt and F. Thompson, Jr., "Collective Bargaining on the Campus: A Survey Five Years After Cornell," 1 *Indus. R. L. J.* 191 (1976) for a recent review of the decisional law.

lems, some of which will be discussed, in practical terms there are today no legislative issues under the National Labor Relations Act since no important effort is being made to amend that statute to deal particularly with the problems of higher education.

The contrary is true with respect to the second kind of legislation: that governing the state public institutions of higher education. Because public employment is not covered by the National Labor Relations Act, those institutions are not subject to the national legislation but constitute a subvariety of public employment governed by state legislation. Collective bargaining in public employment is a rather recent phenomenon and the various states have generated an enormous amount of legislative activity dealing with it. Thus it is in this area that there are presently critical legislative issues. This study will, therefore, focus primarily upon state legislation governing collective bargaining for faculty in public institutions of higher education.

Although we are concerned with public, rather than private, institutions of higher education, we shall try to avoid the vast range of issues that are peculiar to public employment generally but have no special significance for higher education. Questions concerning, for example, the right to strike, the imposition of compulsory arbitration, the authority of subordinate public bodies to make agreements binding the public purse in the absence of the necessary revenue legislation, or the enforcement of collective agreements, are questions which have relevance to all public employment, including higher education. We shall assume, however, that all such problems generic to public employment generally have been resolved in one way or the other and will direct our attention to whether any provisions are required for higher education differing from those applicable to other public employment.

This means that many, although not all, of the considerations we urge would be applicable to special legislation dealing with collective bargaining for faculty in institutions of higher education in the private sector, and we shall draw where appropriate from the experience under the National Labor Relations Act. But there are some problems, such as the concern for the fragmentation of units, that are peculiar to public employment and that, as we shall show, have particular implications for higher education. Thus the essential question, in both public and private employment, is whether there is something particular about faculty collective bargaining that requires special and differing treatment from that accorded to other employees.

The fundamental theme of this study is that there is one aspect of the employment relationship particular to faculty in institutions of higher learning that requires separate treatment in any legislation establishing a system of collective bargaining, particularly for public employees. That aspect, or characteristic, is embodied in systems of academic self-governance. In public as in private employment the common assumption is that in the absence of collective bargaining the employer has the authority both to adopt managerial policy and work rules and to decide, in the first instance, the action necessary to implement them. The introduction of collective bargaining into this kind of employment relationship, whether public or private, only partially modifies this common assumption as to managerial authority. Management may still introduce or change policy but, insofar as the policy or rule concerns subjects within the scope of collective bargaining, it must first bargain with the designated employee representative before doing so. Where rules are agreed upon, or acquiesced in, it remains management's function to manage—to direct the employees, to promote, discharge, or lay them off, and in general to direct the enterprise—and the interests of the employees are expressed in the availability of a grievance procedure to hear complaints that management has violated the rules in performing its functions. The relationship is reflexive: management decides what is to be done, how it is to be done, and by whom, and the collective bargaining representative, if it believes that management has decided in violation of the agreed-upon rules, protests management's action, while complying with it, through the grievance procedure.

In mature institutions of higher education the basic assumption, in the absence of collective bargaining, is contrary to that in other employment. Faculty play a large and often dispositive role in the formulation and implementation of educational policy and in decisions on the selection and retention of faculty members. Thus decisions on what programs of instruction to offer, what students to admit to them, whom to recruit or retain to teach them, or even whether to terminate a program altogether, which in industry would be viewed as the archetypical "management prerogatives" of deciding what to produce, how, and with what labor, are customarily made by the faculty, or only after extensive consultation with it.

The reasons for such faculty participation are closely interrelated. First, decisions of this kind require a high degree of professional expertise; this assumes, rightly, that those most familiar with both the academic discipline and the needs of the institution should participate in the decision-making process. Second, the successful conduct of an academic enterprise requires the active cooperation of the faculty, and the faculty do not regard decisions announced *ex cathedra* as legitimate. Thus even though a particular policy pronouncement or personnel decision, made unilaterally by an administration or governing board, might seem sound to an outside observer, the absence of prior faculty involvement renders the decision suspect to that academic community; the impact of such unilateral action on faculty morale must in turn have a debilitating effect on the success of the institution's academic mission. Finally, the participation of the faculty is one safeguard for academic freedom. Peer participation serves to assure, for example, that a particular program or personnel decision is made on its merits and is not a subterfuge to dispose of a controversial faculty member. As a corollary, the profession has long assumed that academic freedom protects, to some extent, a faculty member's role in institutional governance.

The difference between the more usual employer-employee relationship and the relationship between administration and faculty in higher education has led some to conclude that collective bargaining is simply incompatible with the academic world and that its introduction must necessarily lead to the demise of academic government. We disagree for at least two reasons. First, although faculty members do perform many functions which in the usual employment relationship would be regarded as managerial, they also remain employees. They are, for example, paid salaries, are concerned with pensions and fringe benefits, want adequate working conditions, and need places to park their cars. In most institutions of higher education, these subjects are not collegially governed by the faculty. The absence of collective bargaining thus means the absence of any organized voice for faculty on these nonacademic but important matters.

This consideration is particularly important in the context of the enormous increase in organization among nonacademic state employees with a consequent threat that, unless this increase is countered by academic organization, limited public resources will be diverted to nonacademic employment.

The second reason countering the conclusion that collective bargaining is inconsistent with academic government is empirical. The limited experience of the past few years suggests strongly that, given the appropriate statutory environment, and sometimes even in the absence of that environment, collective bargaining and the traditional form of academic governance can coexist.[3]

The distinctive quality of the employment relationship of faculty does mean, however, that the rules governing other employment relationships shall not be mechanically applied to faculty collective bargaining.[4] Consider, for example, the status of faculty committees, councils, or senates which participate in those management functions that, in academic parlance, are called governance. These faculty agencies are usually supported by the funds of the institution and effectively recommend both the adoption of policies and the action necessary to implement accepted policies. These same organizations, however, represent the interests of faculty as employees. There is no convenient pigeonhole in the traditional labor-management relationship into which these bodies may be placed. On the one hand, in the performance of some of their functions they clearly would fall within the traditional definition of a labor or employee organization and it could be argued, therefore, that the usual prohibition against employer interference or support of a labor or employee organization would prohibit continued financial support for such bodies by the university administration. On the other hand, to the extent that those who participate in these faculty bodies perform management func-

[3]The most recent comprehensive review is F. Kemerer and J. Baldridge, *Unions on Campus* (San Francisco: Jossey-Bass, 1975).

[4]As the chairman of the Michigan Employment Relations Commission recently observed: "The traditional distinction between professional employees in the four-year colleges and universities and similar employees in other enterprises may result in somewhat unique rules for faculty members. This is so because faculty members, since colleges and universities began, have had a significant voice in the determination of policies relating not only to their employment status but also to educational policies." R. G. Howlett, "Overview of State Public Employment Bargaining Legislation: Its History and Present Development," 1 *Okla. City U. L. Rev.* 15, 32 (1976).

tions, such as hiring or firing or effectively recommending the same, those faculty who are members of such bodies may logically be argued to be managerial personnel excluded from the bargaining unit.

There are other problems. Consider, for example, the traditional view, expressed in the 1966 Statement on Government of Colleges and Universities drafted by the American Association of University Professors (AAUP), the American Council on Education (ACE), and the Association of Governing Boards of Universities and Colleges (AGBUC), that faculty have a right to be consulted on the appointment of a university president or chancellor. Under traditional theories, it may very well be argued that insistence on embodiment of such a principle in a collective bargaining agreement would violate the union's duty to bargain, since in the usual employment relationship the choice of management personnel is a matter outside the scope of bargaining. The role of students also presents a special problem. A mechanical transfer of the assumptions of industrial employment would analogize students to consumers entitled to no voice whatsoever in the resolution of disputes between management and employees. But students have increasingly insisted upon, and sometimes achieved, an institutionalized input into the decision-making process. Finally, structuring bargaining and contract administration in a manner most effective for the representative of the employee interests of faculty may weaken the governance system. As a political organization subject to majority rule as well as pressure from interest groups in the unit, engaged in an adversary contest with the employer, the bargaining agency, if improperly structured, may be pushed into agreement to provisions erosive of faculty government in order to secure the greatest good for the greatest number.

It is with concerns of this nature that legislatures must grapple in enacting legislation that would permit collective bargaining in public institutions of higher education. It is our view that the necessary legislative accommodations to the special exigencies of faculty employment can be made, and, indeed, that careful attention to a few particular questions can lay the basis for a successful accommodation of collective bargaining with the traditional form of academic government. We also believe that some of the provisions that have been proposed or enacted, in an effort to deal with the special problems of higher education are unnecessary and harmful. Although these issues will be discussed in detail our three most important recommendations should be noted here.

First, we believe that the single most significant factor in adjusting faculty collective bargaining to higher education lies in the proper definition of the bargaining unit. It is crucial that the unit for the selection of collective bargaining representatives be as congruent as is reasonably possible with the constituency of the existing systems of faculty government. The central problem here, we believe, is to achieve an accommodation between this quintessentially necessary principle and the public employer's interest in a manageable structure for the actual bargaining. We shall propose legislative provisions directed toward meeting these apparently conflicting objectives. Second, we believe that any attempt to limit the scope of bargaining in order to provide separate compartments for academic government and the issues subject to collective bargaining is essentially unworkable and that the scope of bargaining should be sufficiently broad to allow the bargaining agent to achieve an accommodation with institutional government. Third, we believe that the statute must make it clear that internal faculty governing agencies are not labor or employee organizations. Finally, we believe that if the statute is otherwise constructed so as to foster the maintenance of institutions of faculty government, no additional provision need or should be made for some special form of collective bargaining election ballot or for student involvement in the bargaining process.

The discussion will proceed in three parts in the following three chapters. Chapter Two treats those questions posed by state collective bargaining legislation that are of particular concern to institutions of higher learning. The 21 statutes affecting four-year colleges and universities[5] will be discussed, with particular emphasis on those

---

[5]*Alaska Stat.* §§ 23.40.070-23.40.260 (1972); *Conn. P.A.* 566, L. 1975, §§ 1-11; *Del. Code* tit. 19, §§ 1301-1312 (1974); *Fla. Stat.* §§ 447.201-447.607 (1976 Supp.); *Hawaii Rev. Stat.* §§ 89-1-89.20 (1975 Supp.); *Iowa Code* §§ 20.1-20.27 (1976 Supp.); *Kans. Stat.* §§ 75-4321-75-4337 (1975 Supp.); *Me. Rev. Stat.* tit. 26, §§1021-1034 (1975-76 Supp.); *Mass. Gen. Laws* ch. 150E, §§ 1-15 (1976); *Mich Comp. Laws* §§ 423.201-423.216 (1967); *Minn. Stat.* §§ 179.61-179.76 (1976 Supp.); *Mont. Rev. Codes* §§ 59-1601-59-1617 (1975 Cum. Supp.); *Neb. Rev. Stat.* §§ 48-401–48-838 (1974); *N.H. Rev. Stat. Ann.* §§ 273-A:1-273-A.16 (1975): *N.J. Stat.* §§ 34.13A-1-34:13A-11 (1976 Supp.); *N.Y. Civil Service Law* §§ 200-214 (McKinney 1973); *Ore. Rev. Stat.* §§ 243.650-243.782 (1975); *Pa. Stat.* tit. 43, §§ 1101-101–1101.2301 (1976 Supp.); *R.I. Gen. Laws* §§ 36-11-1-3-18-17 (1974); *S.D. Comp. Laws* § 3-18-1-3-18-17 (1974); *Vt. Stat.* tit. 3, §§ 901-1007 (1975).

states that have had substantial experience.[6] Where applicable, these results will be compared with the developments in the private sector under the National Labor Relations Act. Chapter Three contains our recommendations for statutory language. Rather than propose an entire "model" law treating all of the issues relevant to public employment, we have proposed only those sections that we believe are of distinctive concern in connection with faculty collective bargaining. The recommendations will, of necessity, have to be fitted into a much more general scheme of collective bargaining for public employees. Chapter Four presents in tabular form the content of existing state legislation on the more important issues on which we have made recommendations.

[6]The authors particularly wish to thank the following for discussing their views and experiences: Melvin Osterman, Esq., former director of the New York Office of Employee Relations; Howard Rubenstein, counsel, and Leonard Kershaw, assistant director, New York Office of Employee Relations; Vice-Chancellor Jerome Komisar of SUNY; Ralph Dungan, New Jersey Chancellor of Higher Education; President Edward Bloustein of Rutgers; Lewis Kaden, Esq., counsel to Governor Byrne of New Jersey; Don Walters, Esq., provost/director, Massachusetts State College System; and Professor Robert E. Doherty, then advising the Oregon State System of Higher Education.

2

The Salient
Issues

The significant statutory issues for faculty collective bargaining fall under three heads: (1) the definition of the constituency for the representation election, usually identified as unit determination, (2) the structure of bargaining insofar as it transcends the unit, and (3) the scope of bargaining. In addition, attention will be given to special provisions that have been enacted to deal with a student role in collective bargaining and with the representation election ballot. Final comment will be devoted to the question of union security.

I. The Appropriate Bargaining Unit

In the private sector, the National Labor Relations Act provides that the NLRB shall determine the appropriate bargaining unit "in order to assure employees the fullest freedom in exercising the rights" of self-organization and bargaining; that is, the Board must decide whether a particular group of employees is an appropriate one to exercise the right to bargain. The Board need only decide in each case that the unit is appropriate, not that it is the most appropriate or necessarily more appropriate than some other unit. In so doing, it considers a variety of factors such as commonality of employment practices and working conditions, geographic separation, functional integration, degree of interchange among the employees, and "felt" community of interest. The Board may, for example, conclude that an individual plant is an appropriate bargaining unit even though the industrial employer may desire a single unit of all its plants, which could also be appropriate.

However, the actual *structure* of bargaining may transcend the Board's unit determination. The employer and union may negotiate centrally on employerwide policies, even though the union was selected for separate units at each of the employer's plants rather than a single companywide unit, preserving many issues for local settlement. Indeed they may go further and agree to consolidate the units into a single employerwide unit altogether, since that unit would also be appropriate,[7] while preserving local issues for local negotiation.[8] Where more than one union is involved, the parties may agree to negotiate jointly.[9] Should the employer refuse to engage in bargaining with a coalition, members of the coalition may nevertheless sit in on one another's negotiations, although technically only as members of that representative's bargaining team.[10] In sum, as a recent study has pointed out, "current bargaining patterns indicate that the parties 'regularly' shift from an 'appropriate unit' as determined by the Board to a negotiating unit as dictated by the necessities of collective bargaining."[11] Thus the Board is actually deciding upon the appropriate election district for the exercise of the employee's right to select or reject union representation; the unit for which collective bargaining takes place may or may not coincide with the election district.

Contrary to the approach in the private sector, it has been argued that in the public sector only the "most appropriate" unit ought to be determined and that it should be the largest unit feasible.[12] This approach rests on three considerations. First, the diffuson

[7]Owens-Illinois Glass Company, 108 NLRB 947 (1954).

[8]Radio Corp. of America, 135 NLRB 980 (1962).

[9]AFL-CIO Joint Negotiating Committee v. NLRB, 459 F. 2d 374 (3d Cir., 1972).

[10]General Electric Co. v. NLRB, 412 F. 2d 512 (2d Cir. 1969).

[11]J. Abodeely, *The NLRB and the Appropriate Bargaining Unit* (Philadelphia: University of Pennsylvania Press, 1971), p. 6.

[12]See generally the argument and review of authority in E. Rock, "The Appropriate Unit Question in the Public Service: The Problem of Proliferation," 67 *Mich. L. Rev.* 1001 (1969); C. L. Mack "Public Sector Collective Bargaining: Diffusion of Managerial Structure and Fragmentation of Bargaining Units," 2 *Fla. St. U. L. Rev.* 281 (1974);

of managerial authority in public employment among different levels of government requires that the unit be shaped most proximate to that level of government having the power to agree or make effective recommendations on negotiable matters. Second, larger units avoid competition between unions and foster more stable labor relations. Finally, larger units reduce the burdens of negotiation and impasse resolution. In essence, then, this approach proceeds on the assumption that absent a policy requiring the largest feasible bargaining unit the state will simply be incapable of achieving an efficient bargaining structure.

Several of the states surveyed have adopted this policy, usually in the unit determination criteria that the administrative agency must apply, but in three instances by establishing the units legislatively. Hawaii[13] and Maine[14] have mandated a single statewide unit for higher education faculty. Connecticut[15] mandates units for each system (university, state college, community college) under a separate governing board. In these instances the legislatures have misapprehended the nature of the election district decision by confusing it with the actual unit for which bargaining will occur. For the purposes of discussion, however, the common term *bargaining unit* will be used instead of the more precise *election district*.

The assumption that the election and negotiating units should be the same has a special impact on higher education, for it is largely in the public sector that one finds multicampus educational systems governed or coordinated by a single board or department of government. Some contain highly diverse institutions, as in New York, Oregon, Florida, Rhode Island, Kansas, Montana, and Hawaii. Others (such as Minnesota, Connecticut, Massachusetts, New Jersey, and Nebraska state colleges) place institutions of a common educational

---

Final Report, *California Assembly Advisory Council on Public Employee Relations* 84-91 (1973). This approach has been argued specifically in higher education. E. G. Gee, "Organizing the Halls of Ivy: Developing a Framework for Viable Alternatives in Higher Education Employment," 1973 *Utah L. Rev.* 233. See also the thorough treatment provided in Brief for the Florida Board of Regents Re: The Appropriate Bargaining Unit for the State University System (Sept. 4, 1974).

[13]*Hawaii Rev. Stat.* § 89-6(a)(7) (1975 Supp.).

[14]*Me. Rev. Stat. Ann.* tit. 26, § 1024-1A (1975).

[15]*Connecticut P.A.* 566, L. 1975, § 5(b)(4).

level under a single governing or coordinating board, though each institution may lay claim to some distinctiveness and autonomy. Rather than permit each faculty to select an agent responsive to its needs (or to reject collective bargaining altogether) and to permit the parties later to work out a suitable bargaining structure, the mandated identification of the election district with the negotiating unit requires all the faculties (and possibly ancillary professional employees as well) to be lumped together for electoral purposes. As a result, groups with highly diverse traditions and needs will find themselves represented by the one organization able to secure a majority in the election. That organization will then be compelled to reconcile these differences in fashioning its bargaining demands, ordering its priorities, and making trade-offs to achieve a collective agreement. Since the reconciliation will be based to a considerable extent on weight of numbers, the representative's bargaining demands and priorities may not reflect at all, or do so only weakly, the interests of senior faculty, graduate or professional schools, specialized components, or the like. Moreover, the scope of bargaining, no matter how defined (or confined), will perforce affect educational policies; one cannot bargain an agreement on salary levels, hours, and workload without affecting the curriculum. Thus the all-inclusive unit decision may have serious repercussions on the ability of local campuses or special programs to function effectively.

The alternative to this approach is to conform the unit to real community of faculty interest while making special provision to allow the public employer to achieve an efficient bargaining structure, that is, to obviate whipsawing and the burdens of conducting a multiplicity of negotiations on systemwide issues. The first part of this analysis requires discussion of the geographic scope of the unit and the personnel to be included in the unit. The second part will be dealt with separately.

Geographic Scope of Bargaining Unit

The leading decision in support of the more comprehensive unit is that of the New York Public Employment Relations Board (PERB) for the State University of New York.[16] At the time, SUNY consisted

---

[16]State of New York (State University of New York), N.Y. PERB par. 2-3070 (1969).

of 4 university centers, 11 four-year colleges (many former colleges for teacher training), 2 medical centers unaffiliated with a university center, a maritime college, a college of forestry, and 6 two-year agricultural and technical colleges. The structure was described as pyramidal, with the central board exercising general budgetary and policy-making authority. Subject to the Board's general policies, each campus exercised discretion over educational and personnel decisions. Salary maxima by rank were established as a uniform policy, but individual salary decisions were made largely at the campus level. In effect, appointments were effectively made or recommended (depending on the salary of the prospective appointee) at the local level, and tenure was decided centrally, based, however, on local recommendations. The Board policies required each faculty to establish its own system of faculty government. A systemwide senate was also created. Thus the SUNY system, apart from its size, was almost a paradigm for multicampus public higher education, reflecting policies of both central control and institutional diversity and autonomy.

The New York law established three criteria for unit determination: that it shall correspond to a community of employee interest; that it shall be compatible with the joint responsibilities of employer and employees to serve the public; and that "the officials of government at the level of the unit shall have the power to agree, or to make effective recommendations to other administrative authority or the legislative body with respect to the terms and conditions of employment upon which the employees desire to negotiate"[17]—that is, it adopted the policy of the largest feasible unit. Thus the decision of the PERB's director of representation dwelled essentially on this last criterion in concluding that only a single unit was appropriate:

> The power to set general personnel and education policies, fringe benefits, and salary scales, and to determine other economic and non-economic terms and conditions of employment resides in the chancellor or the board of trustees subject, of course, to legislative approval where necessary. Any power the campus presidents have is effectively circumscribed by the existence of the master plan

[17]*N.Y. Civ. Serv. Law* 207-1(b) (McKinney 1973).

and the comprehensive budget for the entire university, both of which are under the control and implementation of the board of trustees. Centralized control of the planning and budget processes also means that almost all allegedly "local" issues will have serious state-wide ramifications, either of an economic or policy nature. For these reasons, it is only during the course of state-wide negotiations with the board of trustees, if at all, that "local" issues could be properly defined and the scope of authority of campus presidents to negotiate on them could be insured. Any attempt to frame local issues independently would be putting the cart before the horse. Until such state-wide negotiations are conducted with a certified employee organization, it is clearly impossible for any sort of meaningful negotiations to take place at the campus level. Thus, the conclusion is inescapable that the establishment of negotiating units on a campus level would run counter to the statutory requirement that a negotiating unit be established at a level where officials of the employer have the power to make determinations or effective recommendations concerning terms and conditions of employment.[18]

The consequences of this policy are illustrated in the conclusion of a recent study of the effects of collective bargaining in SUNY. It is generally conceded that the unit has resulted in a bargaining agent dominated by the two-year and four-year college faculty and the non-teaching support staff.[19] The university-level faculty have had to look to the administration for the protection of their interests rather than to a representative of their own choosing, with varying effect.[20]

[18]State of New York (State University of New York), N.Y. PERB par. 2-4010 at p. 4190 (1969).

[19]E. Duryea and R. Fisk, *Collective Bargaining, the State University and the State Government in New York* (Buffalo: Department of Higher Education, State University of New York, 1975), p. 31: "Fundamentally, PERB's position . . . [on the unit] has intruded a homogenizing influence potentially incompatible to the maintenance of research and scholarly distinction associated with the university centers."

[20]For example, the faculty senate of the University Center at Buffalo prepared an extensive review of the collective agreement and made proposals for bringing it more into

Indeed the medical faculties have conducted what amounts to separate negotiations, albeit under the titular auspices of the overall bargaining agent, in an effort to counteract the effects of the initial unit decision.

The consequences are similarly illustrated in Hawaii, where the legislature mandated that the faculty of the entire system of the University of Hawaii be included in a single unit. This lumped together faculties of a university center, a four-year college, and six community colleges. The divisions between these faculties were reproduced in goals espoused by the organizations they supported.[21] Indeed any agent for so heterogeneous a whole would, in practice, have to arrive through its internal political processes at a bargaining program reconciling the perspectives of meritocratically oriented graduate or professional faculty with the equalitarian demands of junior college faculty. Thus the subsequent history in Hawaii is also instructive. A coalition of two organizations, the local chapter of the AAUP, which was essentially a creature of the university-level faculty, and the National Education Association (NEA), which had been strongest at the four-year college (but with significant support in the two-year institutions), was formed to defeat the incumbent American Federation of Teachers (AFT). It succeeded, but then encountered considerable difficulty in arriving at a uniform negotiating position. In essence the coalition itself, like the separate efforts of the SUNY medical faculties, represented an internal effort within the unit to overcome the ill-advised unit decision. Given the instability inherent in such an arrangement it is not surprising that the final bargaining agreement, embodying the trade-offs the agent was prepared to make, reflected far more the attitude of the equalitarians than the meritocrats.

Quite the contrary approach was taken by the Oregon PERB's hearing officer for that state system, which, while smaller, is essentially similar to SUNY.[22] Under the State Board of Higher Education

---

accord with academic practice at a university level. See Proposals of the SUNY, Buffalo Faculty Senate Committee on Academic Freedom and Responsibility for Revision of the UUP/SUNY Agreement, 1974–1975 (May 19, 1975).

[21] E. Ladd and S. Lipset, *Professors, Unions and American Higher Education* (Berkeley: Carnegie Commission on Higher Education, 1973), Ch. 5.

[22] Oregon State System of Higher Education, Case No. C-277, C-319, C-326, C-375, C-

are nine institutions—the University of Oregon, the Oregon State University, a medical school, a dental school, an urban college (offering some graduate work), a teachers college, two regional liberal arts colleges, and a lower-division technology institution. Like SUNY, the Oregon Board establishes generally applicable uniform policies under which these institutions function. Indeed the hearing officer's report indicates that the degree of detailed regulation by the Oregon Board exceeded that of the SUNY Board. However, the statutory criteria in Oregon are strikingly dissimilar to those in New York, for the Oregon PERB is required to consider "such factors as community of interest, wages, hours and other working conditions of the employees involved, the history of collective bargaining, and the desires of the employees. *The board may determine a unit to be the appropriate unit in a particular case even though some other units might also be appropriate*" [emphasis added].[23]

Thus, unlike New York, the Oregon Board need not define the unit most proximate to the level of government with effective decision-making authority. Indeed the portion of the statute emphasized above reflects an adoption of the private sector approach. Nevertheless, the argument against undue fragmentation had to be confronted.

It is clear that certain matters which are of academic/faculty concern in collective bargaining negotiations can only be effectively negotiated with the Board of Higher Education. This is true with regard to funds allocations, criteria for promotion, criteria for appointments, criteria for awards of tenure, matters involving reduction in force due to program reduction/elimination or financial exigency, and certain statutory or Board granted fringe benefits and privileges. With regard to salaries and statutory retirement and other fringe benefits programs, legislative action would be needed, and negotiations for Board assis-

---

320 (Oct. 31, 1974). The Oregon PERB had earlier determined that a separate unit for one of the system's campuses was appropriate. Southern Oregon College, Ore. PERB No. C-112 (1973).

[23]*Ore. Rev. Stat.* § 243.682(1) (1975).

tance in obtaining implementation of such matters agreed upon would have to take place. However, these negotiations could take place with the Board of Higher Education on all such matters regardless of whether a system-wide or separate campus units exist. The Board has already established an officer to head negotiation teams within the Department of Higher Education, with such teams including executives from affected institutions. *With such a negotiating structure, the Board can bargain with each single institution on all matters whether they affect other institutions or not, and the uniformity of treatment expected or required will result from the Board's spokesman.* While some degree of whipsaw effect can result from negotiations with the separate campus units, this effect can be minimized by coalition efforts and various bargaining ploys. Although testimony was presented to the effect that voluntary coalition did not work in classified bargaining, experience has also shown that academics are extremely capable in accomplishing their objectives. Although some risk of whip-saw exists, such risk does not warrant a disregard of all other factors in the determination of a bargaining unit [emphasis added].[24]

From this perspective the assumption of the New York PERB's director of representation that locally elected agents would negotiate solely with the local campus administration is at odds with the argument that fragmentation will produce whipsawing, which assumes that each local unit deals directly with the central authority. Thus the issue actually posed, as the Oregon Board's hearing officer pointed out, is of structuring the public employer to deal efficiently with representatives elected by and solely responsible to their respective institutional units.

The difference between the New York and Oregon approaches is reflected elsewhere. Pennsylvania,[25] Florida,[26] and Ver-

[24]Oregon State System of Higher Education *supra* note 22 at 38 (memorandum opinion).

[25]*Pa. Stat. Ann.*, tit. 43, § 1101.604(4) (1976 Supp.).

[26]*Fla. Stat. Ann.* § 447.009(4) (1976 Supp.).

mont[27] follow the New York model by legislating against overfragmentation or by requiring the labor board to consider principles of
efficient government administration. Thus it is not surprising that
these state boards have concluded that their respective multicampus
systems compose single bargaining units.[28] However, while Massachusetts[29] and, to a greater extent, Kansas[30] have adopted that policy,
both state labor boards have opted for separate units for the state college and university systems.[31] The Kansas Board relied heavily on the
autonomy afforded each institution, observing that, "The inference
is inescapable that this autonomous relationship is well-known to
faculty members and is a relationship which they approve and foster."[32] Moreover, New Hampshire,[33] Montana,[34] Nebraska[35] and
Rhode Island[36] adopt essentially a community of interest standard.
Those state labor boards have determined that each campus of their
respective multicampus systems represents an appropriate community of interest, and have relied heavily on considerations of educational diversity or institutional autonomy.[37] Similarly, New Jersey

[27]*Vt. Stat. Ann.* tit. 3, § 941(f) (1975).

[28]Re Pennsylvania: Commonwealth of Pennsylvania (13 State Colleges and Indiana
University of Pennsylvania), PERA-R-775 (1971) (single unit stipulated), Pennsyl-
vania State Univ., PERA-R-801 (1973); University of Pittsburgh (Johnstown Campus),
PERA-R-2626 (1973); Re Vermont: Vermont State Colleges, SELRB No. 73-6 (1973); Re
Florida: State Univ. System, Board of Regents, Florida PERC No. 8 H-RC-745-002
(Feb. 5, 1976).

[29]*Mass. Gen. Laws Ann.* ch. 150E, § 3 (1976).

[30]*Kan. Stat. Ann.* § 75-4327(e) (1975 Supp.).

[31]Re Massachusetts: Boston State College, M.L.R.C. No. SCR-35 (1969); Fitchburg
State College, No. ER-151 (1971), Westfield State College, No. ER-184 (1973), Worcester
State College, No. ER-92 (1970), Salem State College [unnumbered] (1973), Re: Kansas:
Kansas State College, Kansas PERB No. UE2-1974 (1974). However, subsequent to the
amendment of the Massachusetts Act, which permits bargaining on economic matters,
a representation petition for the two campuses of the University of Massachusetts
(exclusive of the medical school) has been filed, and it does not appear that any party is
urging a less comprehensive unit.

[32]Kansas State College, *id.* at 4 (memorandum opinion).

[33]*N.H. Rev. Stat. Ann.* § 273-A:8 (1975).

[34]*Mont. Rev. Code Ann.* § 59-1606(2) (1975 Cum. Supp.).

[35]*Neb. Rev. Stat.* § 48-816(2) (1974).

[36]*R.I. Gen. Laws Ann.* § 3-38-15 (1975 Supp.)

[37]Re New Hampshire: University of New Hampshire System, New Hampshire PERB

has adopted a community of interest standard[38] and its somewhat greater experience in the state college system is worth discussing.

In its first confrontation with the issue the New Jersey Public Employment Relations Commission (PERC) created separate units for each of that state's then six state colleges.[39] Each campus was governed by its own board of trustees vested with general authority for the management of the institution. However, the state's Board of Higher Education exercised superior authority in the establishment of uniform policies and guidelines for college administration, including salaries. Noting that the state education law mandated a high degree of self-government for each of the institutions and that the state itself sought separate campus units, the hearing officer stated that

> although there are strong arguments in favor of an overall unit, the argument in favor of separate units is more compelling. We are here concerned with a new development at the colleges. At this stage, care is needed lest the gropings of the faculty to find the most responsive expression of their needs not be crystallized and hardened and frustrate change if that becomes necessary. Once a large unit is established it is difficult to change into smaller units. On the other hand, smaller units may, if it is desired, easily develop into larger units. The smaller units, therefore, would better serve the present interests of the teachers. If an election to determine their choice of organization indicates identical choices at all colleges, a single unit would be the practical result.[40]

N. U-0601 (1976); Re Montana: Northern Montana College, Montana Board of Personal Appeals, Unit Determination No. 55 (1975); Re Nebraska: American Association of University Professors, University of Nebraska v. Board of Regents of the University of Nebraska, Case No. 150 (Nebraska Court of Industrial Relations, 1975); Re Rhode Island: University of Rhode Island, R.I.S.L.R.B. No. EE-1961 (1971), Board of Trustees of State Colleges, R.I.S.L.R.B. No. EE-1845 (1969).

[38]*N.J. Stat. Ann.* § 34:13A-52 (1976 Supp.).

[39]The State Colleges of New Jersey, N. J. PERC No. 1 (1969).

[40]State Colleges of New Jersey, Report and Recommendations of Hearing Officer at 7 (1969) (memorandum opinion).

His prescience was vindicated when each of the campuses selected affiliates of the same organization and negotiated centrally with the Board of Higher Education. A single, comprehensive, systemwide agreement was negotiated. Subsequently a competing organization sought to oust the incumbents on several of the campuses. The state then argued for a single unit. The hearing officer reviewed many of the same facts considered earlier by the PERC as well as the later history of negotiations, the judicial determination that the public employer was the governor, and a later PERC decision favoring larger units. He found a single unit to be appropriate, noting that

> the undersigned would accord greater weight to the policy control which the Board of Higher Education exercises over the colleges than did the Commission [earlier]. . . . [T]he factors cited by the Commission . . . a measure of local autonomy, day-to-day supervision from the individual colleges, and the fact that each college affects the tenure of its staff and each governs their working conditions—can be accommodated within the structure of a statewide bargaining unit.[41]

The perspectives underlying these two decisions differ significantly, wholly apart from the politically persuasive, if not dispositive, shift in position of the public employer. The former tends to view the issue as the establishment of an election district that need not be extensive with the bargaining structure that will actually result. The public policy favoring autonomy and a large degree of local campus government militated toward separate campus election districts. The latter accepts the argument that in the public sector unit determination and bargaining structure should be coextensive. It does so, moreover, based on a concern for fragmentation established by the PERC itself and not on any such policy explicitly embodied in the statute, which merely requires that the unit be defined "with due regard for the community of interest among the employees concerned."

[41]State of New Jersey, PERC No. 72, Hearing Officer's Report and Recommendations at 14 (1972) (memorandum opinion).

On the other hand, the second PERC decision can be read as being consistent with the private sector approach, for there had been a history of actual bargaining on a systemwide basis by the single organization selected in each of the local election districts, and a comprehensive systemwide contract had been agreed to. Thus the decision actually represents a consolidation of appropriate bargaining units into a single bargaining unit, also appropriate, on the basis of bargaining history.

The muddling of the concepts of bargaining unit, election district, and bargaining structure is nowhere better reflected than in the Minnesota Act. The criteria for unit determination include geographic location and "place particular importance upon the history and extent of organization and the desires of the petitioning employee representatives."[42] Since the clearest community of interest under these criteria is at the campus level, this would seem to create a presumption in favor of campus units. However, a later section requires the relevant administrative agency to "define appropriate units of state employees as all the employees under the same appointing authority except where professional, geographical or other considerations affecting employment relations clearly require appropriate units of some other composition."[43]

Thus, for state employees, the presumption created by this section is struck the other way. The seemingly conflicting language had to be applied to the state college system, comprising seven institutions governed by a single state college board. Unlike the New Jersey state colleges, the legislation governing the state college system did not reflect a policy favoring diversity and self-governance at the local level. Nevertheless the state college board itself had adopted a lengthy set of rules that established considerable discretion and autonomy for the individual campus. Given the unit determination criteria, the threshold question was the determination of the "appointing authority" and, if central, whether the "other considerations" militated nevertheless toward separate units. The Minnesota PERB held 3-2 for separate campus units,[44] concluding that in view of the extensive

[42]*Minn. Stat.* § 179.71(3) (1976 Supp.).

[43]*Minn. Stat.* § 179.74(4) (1976 Supp.).

[44]Minnesota State College Board, Minnesota PERB Nos. 72-PR-180-A, 73-PR-414-A, 73-PR-431-A (1974) (memorandum opinion).

delegation of authority at the local level, the appointing authority was effectively the local campus president. Alternatively, it held that in any event local units were mandated by consideration of the additional criteria:

> In brief, the record clearly indicates that the totality of the web of professional and employment relationships for a faculty member is woven and set in a given State College. The legal relationships and pragmatic, operational arrangements evidence *seven* State College faculties, rather than *a* faculty for the State Colleges.
>
> For all of the above facts, the faculty members of each State College warrant the opportunity to "choose freely their representatives." This statutory right is a necessary condition for the development of responsible and effective collective bargaining. This right could be denied the faculty members of a given (and, especially, a smaller) State College if their views were submerged within a state-wide unit. On the other hand, should the various faculties prefer a broader unit, they would be free, within the scope of the above Decision, to exercise such option through the electoral process [emphasis in original].[45]

One dissenting member simply disagreed that the delegation effectively disestablished the central board as the "appointing authority." The second dissenter, Member Obermeyer, disagreed more extensively on the effects of overfragmentation.[46] The Su-

[45]*Id.* at 6.

[46]*Id.* at 6:

> The ultimate objective of this Board should be the establishment of appropriate bargaining units which promote stability, within the statutory alternatives available, between public employers and exclusive representatives of their employees— not the establishment of units which offer conflict possibilities.
>
> In my judgment, a state-wide determination provides the vehicle for providing this stability. A state-wide unit reduces the availability of the "whip saw" tactic on the part of the exclusive representative or the employer while also providing for the establishment of *consistent* "terms and conditions of employment." The majority alleges that its determination is appropriate because "[t]he colleges are distinct, self-contained operating entities" with varying "educational programs" and a system of governing through individual "constitutional arrangements" which results

preme Court of Minnesota sided with the dissenters on both grounds.[47]

However, the Minnesota Act attempts to reconcile the public employer's need for an efficient bargaining structure with the community of interest criteria embodied in the Act, which militates toward less than comprehensive units: "Regardless of unit determination the governor may upon the unanimous written request of exclusive representatives of units and appointing authorities direct that negotiations can be conducted for one or more appointing authorities in a common proceeding."[48] The Minnesota court acknowledged the argument that this provision eroded the assertion that local units would produce an unstable or unduly fragmented bargaining structure but simply declined to distinguish that provision or otherwise confront the argument.

More recently, the Minnesota PERB refused to follow the state's supreme court in considering the unit determination for the University of Minnesota. It held that each of the university's five campuses was an appropriate unit.[49] The Board distinguished the state college decision on grounds that the statutory provision with respect to the "appointing authority" was inapplicable to the university. Thus it relied heavily on the autonomy and educational distinctiveness of each of the campuses as well as geographic separation, in its decision. Moreover, the Board pointed out that the community of interest and faculty organizational structure of the main campus would be preserved by the decision "without submerging the frequently distinct interests of their less numerous colleagues on the coordinate campuses."[50] Member Obermeyer dissented.

---

in the "totality of the web of professional and employment relationships for a faculty member [which] is woven and set in a given college." The crucial issue still exists, however, what unit determination will best promote a stable relationship between the State College Board and the Professional Teaching Staff if they choose to be represented by a "labor or employee organization?" [emphasis in original].

[47]Minnesota State College Bd. v. Public Employment Relations Bd., 228 N. W. 2d 551 (Minn. 1975).

[48]*Minn. Stat.* § 179.74(4) (1976 Supp.).

[49]University of Minnesota Board of Regents, Minnesota PERB Case Nos. 73-PR-571A, 74-PR-59-A, 74-PR-66-A, 74-PR-93A (1975).

[50]*Id.* at 13 (memorandum opinion).

The difference between the majority and Member Obermeyer in the *Minnesota State College* and *University of Minnesota* cases reflects the critical distinction between *bargaining structure* and *election district*. Under a separate campus election unit structure, the agents selected owe a direct obligation to their local constituencies. While a statutory effort is made more explicitly to allow centralized administration to rationalize its bargaining program, each agent nevertheless retains independent authority over local and perhaps unique bargaining subjects. As the SUNY and Hawaii experience suggests, an agent certified for a local campus may have greater bargaining power in reaching an accommodation with other agents on systemwide issues than a minority faculty group has in dealing with a single organization certified to represent a rather diverse whole. Thus where the policy of the state embodied in law or practice is to encourage a degree of local autonomy or educational diversity, an initial single-unit decision may be highly detrimental to that goal.

Occupational Scope

The question of what jobs are to be included in the bargaining unit presents, on a more refined scale, the same issue. Not only will occupants of the jobs included in the unit have a say in the selection of the agent, but their interests must also be fairly represented at the bargaining table. Moreover, as noted earlier, the collective agreement will affect educational policy and program decisions. Thus it becomes crucial that an essentially academic focus not be blurred either by the inclusion of nonacademics or by the exclusion of academic colleagues under the rubric of a supervisory or managerial exemption; that is, the polity for the selection of the bargaining agent must be essentially coextensive with the polity in the system of academic government.

The National Labor Relations Act forbids the inclusion of nonprofessionals in a unit with professionals unless the latter vote for the inclusion. Although not every state act explicitly so provides, in no case have nonprofessional employees been included with the faculty for bargaining purposes. Of concern is the status of nonteaching professional (or semiprofessional) employees, part-time faculty, graduate students, the faculties of professional schools, and supervisory or managerial employees.

NONTEACHING PROFESSIONALS

Many of the arguments urged on behalf of systemwide units are mustered in support of the inclusion of ancillary professional (and semi-professional) positions with the core faculty: they further the general educational mission of the institution (and in that capacity interact with students and faculty); some terms and conditions of employment may be common to both groups; there is no patent conflict of interests between them; and, in the absence of such conflict, public policy should favor larger bargaining units in the public sector.

Accordingly, the Michigan Employment Relations Commission (MERC) declined to accept its trial examiner's exclusion of non-faculty from the faculty bargaining unit at Eastern Michigan and Wayne State universities.[51] In *Wayne State*, the trial examiner had reasoned that:

> The primary distinction separating the teaching faculty from the academic staff is based upon their job function which is directed primarily at classroom teaching. The teaching faculty have historically been treated differently from the other University personnel with regard to wages, hours, and working conditions. Thus, while by no means universal, the teaching faculty are generally expected to attain a higher degree of educational achievement, such as the attainment of a doctorate degree, than is required for other University personnel, including academic staff; scholarly research and publication is a common expectation of a teaching faculty position; the salary system of the teaching faculty based upon the four traditional ranks is substantially different from other University personnel; the working hours and work year of the teaching faculty differs considerably from other University personnel in that their hours of service at the University depend upon their classroom and other assignments, which can be either during the normal work day or in the evening and

[51] Eastern Michigan University, MERC Case Nos. R70K-407, R71-A-2 (1972), Wayne State University, MERC Case Nos. R71B-58, R71B-75, R71B-79, R71C-137 (1972).

which vary considerably from day to day; the service year for teaching faculty is usually based on a nine months basis rather than twelve months as are other employees; and the teaching faculty have unique responsibilities in determining the makeup of the curriculum, requirements for graduation, recommending hiring and promotion of fellow members of the department, and other direct participation in what are normally considered management functions; and they are given the traditional protection of tenure, whereas the remaining professional staff is granted "continuing service" status by the University.[52]

The trial examiner amplified this somewhat in the *Eastern Michigan* decision, which dwelled on the faculty's special responsibilities for the academic program and the resulting structure of internal governance particular to the faculty and not shared with nonfaculty:

The structure of collegiality recognized by the major universities is limited to its teaching faculty who are in what is called the tenure chain. This unique structure, along with the fact that teaching faculty have a separate wage structure, and their working conditions and hours vary considerably from other University employees, makes for a community of interest separate from other employees of the University. These employees represent a clearly identifiable unit with common interests and working conditions which, in the main, are not shared by other professional or administrative positions within the University. Further, an extension of the unit beyond those primarily engaged in teaching opens up serious problems as to the extent of a bargaining unit in a major university, where the multiplicity of classifications and employees in such classifications who perform functions auxiliary to teaching makes it difficult, if not impossible, to appropriately define a bar-

[52]Wayne State University *id.* Report of Trial Examiner at 9 (memorandum opinion).

gaining unit with a commonality of wages, hours, and working conditions.[53]

The MERC rejected these arguments.

> A bargaining unit in a major university should not be limited to faculty members of demonstrably diverse professional and intellectual interests. The extensive supporting professional staff at the University should bargain with the general faculty. *Accord, State Univ. of New York*, ... The supporting staff and faculty are functionally integrated groups by virtue of their synergistic efforts aimed at the education of University students.
>
> A community of interest exists between the various professional groups which the labor organizations seek to include within one bargaining unit. This relationship arises out of one of the major aims of the University. The record disclosed that a primary purpose of the University is to educate and prepare students for the eventual roles that they will lead in life. This educational process is the central focus of the activities of *both* the faculty and the several classes of advisors and counselors [emphasis in original].[54]

The MERC decision in *Eastern Michigan* was reversed by the state court of appeals largely because the conclusion was not supported in the trial examiner's findings of fact, which the Commission had adopted.[55] Nevertheless, the MERC's reasoning is noteworthy for the extensive treatment given the issue. A similar all-inclusive approach has been taken by the New York PERB in SUNY[56] and the New Jersey PERC[57] for that state college system.

[53]Eastern Michigan University *supra* note 51, Report of Trial Examiner at 8-9 (memorandum opinion).

[54]Eastern Michigan University *supra* note 51 at 4-5 (memorandum opinion). It reversed in Wayne State solely on the basis of the Eastern Michigan decision.

[55]Board of Regents of Eastern Michigan University v. Eastern Michigan University Chapter, American Ass'n of University Professors, 46 Mich. App. 534, 208 N.W. 2d 641 (1973).

[56]State of New York (State University of New York), *supra* note 16.

[57]The State Colleges of New Jersey, *supra* note 39. Note the reasoning of the hearing

In the private sector, however, the NLRB has taken an approach rather different from that embraced by the New York, New Jersey, and Michigan boards. Although in some of its very early decisions it seemed to accept the inclusion of all professionals, broadly defined, with the faculty, as its experience grew it began to refine the concept of professionalism. It now requires that the statutorily mandated advanced education be related to the professional work performed and that the work itself be related to a discipline or field of science within the purview of the teaching profession.[58] Thus many of the administrative positions included in the public sector would be excluded in private higher education as being either nonprofessional or lacking community of interest with the faculty.

Subsequent to the refinement of NLRB law in the private sector, the status of nonfaculty support staff was again presented to the New York PERB's director of representation by a petition for separate representation.[59] Unlike the first case, the public employer took no official position. Nevertheless the director refused to separate nonfaculty from the faculty. He continued to reason that, in view of the PERB's policy in favor of larger units, nonacademics would be separated only if a conflict between the two groups could be proved. Accordingly he reviewed the evidence of the disputes between the two groups in establishing negotiating goals and in the conduct of bargaining and concluded that a "commendable spirit of compromise" prevailed.

Understandably, in order to ascertain whether there was a conflict that justified separate unit treatment, the director attended

---

officer in the New Jersey State College case, *supra* note 41 at 11-12 (memorandum opinion):

> It is my opinion that the appropriate unit should not be so narrow as to include only the teaching staff. The administrative staff and the educational support staff have parallel interests which do not conflict with and are not adverse to the interests of the teaching faculty. If the unit is determined only by the narrowest congruent interests, the result may be so many separate units that organization would become a practical impossibility for some groups. *It would be better to lump all professional groups at each college excluding those whose interests are fundamentally conflicting* [emphasis added].

[58] This summary is based on the fuller analysis supplied in Finkin, *supra* note 2.

[59] State of New York (State University of New York), NY PERB No. C-0991 (Jan. 21, 1974) (decision of Director of Representation). The decision was not appealed to the PERB.

almost entirely to whether the interests of the nonfaculty minority were roughly dealt with, but the decision failed to come to grips with the political realities created by the earlier unit decision.

Given the divisions within the faculty, the nonacademics represented a "swing vote" in the election, which they used to bargain for greater representation in the affairs of the bargaining agent than their numbers would otherwise dictate. The result was a contract concerned more with their interests than with those of the core faculty, especially at the university level. As Joseph Garbarino pointed out, at SUNY and elsewhere: "The paradox of faculty unionism to date is that the greatest gains have accrued to the teaching faculty on the margin of the core faculty, to the faculty of the institutions in the integrated systems that have been lowest in the academic hierarchy, and to the nonfaculty professionals."[60]

Closely related, it appears from the decision that the nonacademics bargained with factions in the academic group to achieve a bargaining consensus. On issues of job security or tenure, for example, the nonacademics seem to have allied themselves with a faction of nontenured faculty, thereby outvoting tenured faculty on that bargaining demand. Thus the inclusion of nonacademics in the bargaining unit gave them an important voice in matters affecting the faculty in which they had no valid interest. For the most part, however, it appears that units in public higher education have tended to be limited to the core faculty.[61]

PART-TIME FACULTY AND GRADUATE ASSISTANTS

Accepting much of the foregoing analysis, the NLRB has tended to shape bargaining units to conform essentially to the core teaching and research faculty and those few professionals, for example, librarians, who share most directly in the conduct of the educational mis-

[60] J. W. Garbarino, "Faculty Unionism: From Theory to Practice," 11 *Indus. Rel.* 1, 15 (1972).

[61] In one of the few contested cases the Pennsylvania Labor Relations Board excluded nonteaching professionals in University of Pittsburgh, note 66 *infra*. Units limited to faculty rank include the University of Nebraska, *supra* note 37, Kansas State College, *supra* note 32, University of New Hampshire, *supra* note 37, University of Delaware, *infra* note 85, University of Rhode Island, *supra* note 37, Vermont State Colleges, Vermont SELRB Direction of Election (Sept. 25, 1973), and the Massachusetts State Colleges, *supra* note 31.

sion. However, the status of part-time faculty has posed a significant issue for the Board because its industrial precedents accord voting status to all but the casual or purely temporary employee, and the private urban university tends to employ large numbers of part-time faculty who teach on a fairly regular basis. Moreover, it is easy to view a part-timer who teaches two courses as doing half the work of a full-timer who teaches four. Thus it becomes attractive, at least superficially, to assume that the two have similar qualifications, perform similar work and share a community of interest.

While the Board accepted this conclusion in its early confrontation with the question, it later reversed itself and concluded that only those part-timers eligible for academic tenure would be included with the full-time faculty.[62] While the early decisions were clearly very broad, the later rule appears rather rigid, inasmuch as some full-time faculty, for example, research professors, may be ineligible for tenure, and some part-timers may participate very directly in institutional governance. Nevertheless, the rule is easy to apply and does at least roughly approximate a unit geared to central academic values.

The issue has proved less contentious in the public sector, perhaps because many public institutions are nonurban and, lacking an available local labor pool, tend not to employ a sufficient number of part-timers to give rise to disputes over their status.[63] The state board decisions in contested cases reflect acceptance of one or the other of the arguments made before the NLRB: that more stable and rational labor relations require the inclusion of regular part-timers, or that the existing constituency for internal faculty government (which usually excludes part-timers) should largely determine the constituency for bargaining. Thus the MERC included regular part-timers at Wayne State University,[64] but the New Jersey PERC excluded them in the New Jersey State Colleges.[65]

[62]New York University, 205 NLRB No. 16 (1973). A fuller history is provided in Finkin, *supra* note 2.

[63]Pennsylvania State Colleges, *supra* note 28 (inclusion of regular part-timers agreed to), Southern Oregon College, *supra* note 22 (half-time status agreed to), Massachusetts State Colleges, *supra* note 31 (part-timers excluded), Vermont State Colleges, *supra* note 28 (part-timers excluded), University of Rhode Island, *supra* note 37 (part-timers excluded).

[64]Wayne State University, *supra* note 51.

[65]New Jersey State Colleges, *supra* note 39.

The similarity of functions, viewed solely as teaching, would logically also lead to the inclusion of graduate teaching or research assistants in faculty bargaining units. The NLRB has viewed them as students, lacking a community of interest with the faculty, and has excluded them from a faculty unit. The public sector decisions have allowed them to bargain but in no case have they been included with the faculty by labor board decision.[66]

PROFESSIONAL SCHOOLS

The NLRB has permitted the faculties of law schools to vote separately on whether to be included in or excluded from larger campus units as well as to vote on representation.[67] The Board has relied on differences in salary, separate accreditation, physical location, professional identification, calendar, and the like in arriving at that result, and has recognized that such differences may be applicable to other professional schools as well. Thus it has given similar treatment to the School of Medicine and the School of Marine and Atmospheric Science of the University of Miami.[68]

The NLRB's reasoning was followed by the Pennsylvania Labor Relations Board, which allowed the medical, dental and law schools of Temple University to separate themselves from the rest of the university faculty;[69] by the Minnesota Board, which separated the schools of law and health sciences (but not the College of Veterinary Medicine) from the faculty unit at the main campus;[70] and by the Nebraska Court of Industrial Relations, which separated the University of Nebraska's schools of law and dentistry.[71] Similarly, the Florida PERB established separate units for that system's law schools, the health center, and the Institute of Food and Agricultural Sciences at the University of Florida, but it declined to establish a

[66]See, for example, University of Pittsburgh, PLRB Case Nos. PERA-R-5237-W *et al.* (1976).

[67]New York University, *supra* note 62, Syracuse University, 204 NLRB No. 85 (1973).

[68]University of Miami, 231 NLRB No. 64 (1974).

[69]Temple University, PERA-R-1123E, 1137-E (1972). To the same effect see University of Pittsburgh, *supra* note 66 (separate units for law, medicine, and the school of health professions).

[70]University of Minnesota, *supra* note 49.

[71]AAUP v. Board of Regents of the University of Nebraska, *supra* note 37.

separate unit for engineering faculty.[72] The Michigan Employment Relations Commission included the medical faculty in the broader unit at Wayne State University.[73]

The debate on the status of professional schools rehearses much of the argument on the status of educationally diverse, geographically dispersed campuses, albeit on a smaller scale. The disciplinary group may resent having to filter its demands through a universitywide agent and may fear that matters of special concern will be traded off by the larger collective, thus impairing its morale and conceivably its ability to perform satisfactorily. On the other hand, inclusion may compel professional school faculties to interest themselves in the affairs of the larger collective, perhaps reducing the parochialism of professional education. In addition, while these faculties doubtless represent a separate community of interest, they often participate in campus governance and thus also share a wider community of interest. Moreover, the NLRB's position that a law, medical, or marine science school represents "an identifiable group of employes whose separate community of interest is not irrevocably submerged in the broad community of interest which they share with other faculty" palpably may also apply to other disciplinary components of a large university.

Here, as elsewhere, it is important to distinguish between situations in which the only question is whether the unit sought is an appropriate one so that an election may be held despite the argument that only an overall unit is permissible,[74] and the situation in which competitive petitions require the determination of the more appropriate of the two differing units sought. In the latter situation the NLRB recognizes that an inclusive unit and separate units are equally appropriate and thus defers to the judgment of the professional school faculty.

The justification of this approach, which might commend itself to labor boards in the public sector where either of two units would be appropriate under established community of interest criteria,[75] must lie in the structure of academic government in the par-

[72]State University System, Board of Regents, *supra* note 28.

[73]Wayne State Univ., *supra* note 51.

[74]See, for example, Fordham University, 193 NLRB 134 (1971).

[75]The Vermont Act provides *inter alia* that "a secret ballot election shall be conducted by the board to be taken in such manner as to show separately the wishes of the employees in the voting group involved as to the determination of the collective bargaining

ticular university. If the professional school is fully integrated into that structure, with its appointments, curriculum, admissions standards, and the like subject to the same or similar academic control mechanisms as other disciplines and if its faculty participates fully in campus collegial governance, there seems no reasonable basis to permit self-determination elections for law, medical, or marine science schools and not for other specialized disciplines. If, on the other hand, as appears often to be the case, the academic government of these schools is substantially divorced from that of the rest of the university and has a degree of autonomy from the controls exercised by centralized faculty bodies over other disciplines, the difference may be justified. The key here, as elsewhere, is to permit the election district to be set up in the fashion that best fits the existing structure of academic government.[76]

MANAGERS AND SUPERVISORS

As a result of successful efforts by rank-and-file unions to organize plant foremen and the resulting alarm in the business community, the National Labor Relations Act was amended in 1947 to exclude supervisors from the category of employees entitled to a protected right to organize and bargain. A supervisor is defined as

> any individual having authority, in the interest of the employer, to hire, transfer, suspend, lay off, recall, promote, discharge, assign, reward, or discipline other employees, or responsibly to direct them, or to adjust their grievances, or effectively to recommend such action, if in connection with the foregoing the exercise of such

---

unit...." *Vt. Stat. Ann.* § 941(e) (1975). However, this language has been interpreted as applying to the representation election ballot rather than to unit determination. See section IV(B) *infra*.

[76]Although we think the principle is clear, the line to be drawn may not be. In *Fordham*, a noncompetitive case, there was substantial autonomy as to courses and curriculum, but the law school faculty members served "on the Faculty Senate and other University committees," a factor that might well have argued for an inclusive unit determination in a competitive case. In *Syracuse University*, on the other hand, the Board found that the law school was "virtually autonomous, subject only to University's basic administrative rules and regulations."

authority is not of a merely routine or clerical nature, but requires the use of independent judgment.[77]

At the same time the Act was also amended to make clear that professional employees were entitled to separate representation unless they chose otherwise. A professional is defined as

(a) any employee engaged in work (i) predominately intellectual and varied in character as opposed to routine mental, manual, mechanical, or physical work; (ii) involving the consistent exercise of discretion and judgment in its performance; (iii) of such a character that the output produced or the result accomplished cannot be standardized in relation to a given period of time; (iv) requiring knowledge of an advanced type in a field of science or learning customarily acquired by a prolonged course of specialized intellectual instruction and study in an institution of higher learning or a hospital, as distinguished from a general academic education or from an apprenticeship or from training in the performance of routine mental, manual, or physical processes; or

(b) any employee, who (i) has completed the courses of specialized intellectual instruction and study described in clause (iv) of paragraph (a), and (ii) is performing related work under the supervision of a professional person to qualify himself to become a professional employee as defined in paragraph (a).[78]

Given the legislative history of this provision and the fact that professional work invariably entails supervisory responsibilities, there is a latent tension in the exclusion of supervisors and the inclusion of professionals, which has been, in effect, delegated to the labor board for resolution.

Moreover, the federal act nowhere speaks explicitly to the status of managerial personnel. The Supreme Court has made clear that

[77]29 U.S.C. § 152(11) (1970).

[78]29 U.S.C. § 152(12) (1970).

managerial personnel must be excluded from the Act's coverage.[79] Lacking an explicit statutory definition, the standards of managerial status are considerably more vague than the test for supervisory status.

Inasmuch as the faculty often plays a significant role in educational decision-making and in decisions on the selection, retention, and promotion of colleagues, several institutional administrations have argued that their faculties have a managerial or supervisory character and thus should be denied the statutory right to bargain. The NLRB has rejected these arguments, viewing the faculty's role as advisory rather than managerial and as being inextricably interwoven with the kind of professional work the faculty performs.[80] No similar arguments have been made in the public sector even though faculty there may enjoy an explicit policy-making role by statute or delegation.

In the public sector, state legislatures must decide whether they wish to follow the federal model and exclude supervisory and managerial personnel altogether, to allow either or both to form separate bargaining units independent of the rank-and-file, or to allow either or both to be included in bargaining units with the rank-and-file. While analysis of that general policy question is beyond the scope of this study, a decision to exclude supervisors or managers from rank-and-file units may pose a problem for the leaders of academic programs, for example, department chairmen, division directors, or program coordinators, who may ostensibly exercise such authority. Academic observers who have examined this issue generally agree that to exclude those who are primarily academics under the rubric of a supervisory or managerial exemption will rend the fabric of collegial relations within the program, deprive both the faculty and its collective representative of its accustomed leadership and, over time, erode the quality of the program at least insofar as the health of collegial relations in the academic unit affects the educational mission.[81]

---

[79]Bell Aerospace Co., Division of Textron, Inc. v. NLRB, 416 U.S. 267 (1974).

[80]The cases are discussed in Finkin, *supra* note 2 at 612–618. More recently see Northeastern University, 218 NLRB No. 40 (1975).

[81]Finkin, *supra* note 2 at 635–636, R. Carr and D. Van Eyck, *Collective Bargaining Comes to the Campus* (Washington, D.C.: American Council on Education, 1973), pp. 112–114.

The NLRB has, if haltingly, recognized the significance of the issue. In its earliest decisions the Board found effective recommendatory power over in-unit personnel, without more, sufficient to establish supervisory status. The Board did, in some cases, decline to find supervisory status where the recommendations of the program leader were not "effective," that is, where they were subject to additional review and had occasionally been reversed. More recently, however, the Board has examined whether the chairman possesses "individual" authority or instead serves as the spokesman for the academic peer group, and even where he functions individually whether he does so "in the interest of the employer" or on behalf of his peers, acting, in a sense, by delegation from them and occasionally at variance with the expressed desires of higher authority.[82] While this reading of the supervisory exemption is perhaps technical, it is consistent with Board decisions affecting other professionals and is clearly responsive to the academic setting.

Decisions in the public sector reflect either the mechanical approach of the NLRB's earliest cases or the more refined analysis of its later ones. Thus the Michigan Employment Relations Commission excluded department chairmen at Eastern Michigan University and Wayne State University, relying in both cases on the recommendations of its trial examiner.[83] In the latter case, the trial examiner observed:

> The major problem as to department chairmen is the fact that their decisions and recommendations, and even the choice of a chairman himself, are reached frequently through the collegial decision-making process peculiar to higher education. . . .
>
> [Nevertheless] I conclude that the department chairmen have and exercise the authority to make effective recommendations as to the hiring and change of status of faculty members and other employees of the University.

[82]The divided lines of Board authority are discussed in Finkin, *supra* note 2 at 632–640. The Board has continued to adhere to these inconsistent lines of authority. *Compare* Yeshiva University, 221 NLRB No. 169 (1975) *with* University of Vermont and State and Agricultural College, 223 NLRB No. 46 (1976).

[83]Eastern Michigan Univ., *supra* note 51, Wayne State Univ., *supra* note 51.

Thus, while the department chairmen usually consult their colleagues . . . [they] are expected to and do make their own decisions which can effectively overrule departmental recommendations.[84]

In essence, the trial examiner declined to examine the question of on whose behalf the chairmen really functioned even when exercising independent judgment. Similarly, the Kansas PERB agonized over the dual role of the department chairmanship at Kansas State College of Pittsburg, and the Delaware agency merely mentioned the issue for the University of Delaware, but both came down in favor of supervisory status.[85]

In Temple University, however, the Pennsylvania Labor Relations Board clearly adhered to the NLRB's more sophisticated analysis.[86] Applying a similar approach, chairmen have been held to be

[84]Wayne State Univ., *supra* at 20, 21–22.

[85]Kansas State College, *supra* note 31, Delaware Department of Labor Case No. 111 (1972). In addition, the hearing officer in the first decision for the New Jersey state colleges was required to segregate supervisors into a separate unit. His remarks were clearly directed to department chairpersons:

> My recommendation is that they be excluded. I recognize that there are important differences between supervision in the private sector and in the public sector, and especially in the field of higher education. Self-governance and peer judgment undoubtedly diffuse the impact that supervisors have upon members of the negotiating unit. Academic freedom and professionalism also play a part in making the faculty less sensitive to the conflicting interest of their supervisors. Nevertheless, a conflict of interest does exist. The teacher is responsible to his supervisor who is, in turn, accountable for his subordinates. These duties and obligations often give rise to grievances in which the negotiating representative may be called upon to participate. Obviously, it cannot be on both sides of such a conflict. It is this conflicting interest which requires that supervisors be excluded from the unit.

Report of Hearing Officer, *supra* note 40 at 11. The PERC delegated the resolution to a challenge-ballot proceeding. Chairmen were explicitly included in the later direction of election. The New Jersey State Colleges, *supra* note 39.

[86]Temple University, *supra* note 69. The PLRB said:

> In our view a first level supervisor must act on "behalf of the Employer" in hiring, transferring, suspending, laying off, recalling, promoting, discharging, assigning, rewarding, disciplining other employes or effectively being able to recommend such action. The touchstone here is the word "on behalf of the Employer." The evidence adduced in this record shows that the departmental chairman operates on behalf of the employes as often as he does or more often than he does on behalf of the Employer. In addition, he never acts between members of the faculty. A departmental chairman would not dare to observe the performance of the teachers in his

nonsupervisory at the University of Nebraska,[87] the University of New Hampshire,[88] the University of Rhode Island,[89] and Southern Oregon College,[90] and were held to be nonmanagerial at the University of Hawaii.[91] Thus the weight of decided cases in the public sector has favored the better NLRB approach.

II. The Structure of Bargaining

The foregoing has suggested that the widely accepted policy requiring the largest feasible bargaining units in public employment will, if followed in higher education, produce results contrary to the interests of the affected institutions. As the discussion of scope of bargaining will show, it is imperative that the faculty's governance constituency coincide with the constituency that selects a bargaining agent if there is to be a satisfactory accommodation between the two. Nevertheless, the strong justification for larger units is the need to create a structure of bargaining that will reduce whipsawing and foster stable labor relations. In lieu of all-encompassing bargaining units, this may be achieved by treating the structure of bargaining directly.

---

department in a reporting sense, and would not visit a class conducted by a member of the department unless invited to do so. At the most, the departmental chairman argues with the dean for more money for the whole department, but in these days of shortages, is usually used by the dean to placate department members and to explain why more money is not available for the department. No department chairman assigns work, and his recommendation power is generally no greater than the faculty members or faculty committees. The very loose and diverse manner in which department chairmen are assigned and picked would mediate against finding that they operate on behalf of the Employer. The best that can be said is that the departmental chairman absorbs his knowledge of his department by osmosis and transmits it in the same way. It is our view that the most effective recommendation of power in the University starts at the dean's level and we have been urged to adopt the National Board's views expressed in the Fordham Case, but again we state that where the facts were so similar we will adopt the same rationale in reaching the similar conclusion. *Id.* at 8 (memorandum opinion).

Nevertheless, the PLRB reached a contrary conclusion in University of Pittsburgh, *supra* note 66.

[87]AAUP v. Board of Regents of the University of Nebraska, *supra* note 37.

[88]University of New Hampshire, *supra* note 37.

[89]University of Rhode Island, *supra* note 37.

[90]Southern Oregon College, *supra* note 22.

[91]University of Hawaii, H. PERB No. R-07-12 (1972).

One such approach, adopted by several states, is to treat with the question of bargaining structure by identifying the "public employer," that is, the "management" with which the union must deal, as the state's chief executive or the board of trustees of the college or university system. Montana designates its Commissioner of Higher Education as the employer's representative.[92] New Hampshire goes further by legislatively establishing the composition of the employer's central negotiating committee.[93] These efforts clarify with whom the bargaining agent must treat and anticipate central negotiations on matters of systemwide concern. However, central bargaining on such matters would occur even in the absence of a statutory provision and, as a possible approach to bargaining structure, these provisions fail to take account of two considerations. First, who the "public employer" is, just as who the employer is in the private sector, varies with the issue presented. For an employee of a large conglomerate, for example, the "employer" with whom his union must deal may vary from the foreman to a national representative of the company, depending upon the issue. So, too, in public employment. The "employer" of a faculty member may be his or her dean, the campus president, the system's chancellor, the state's office of employee relations, or the legislature, depending, again, on the issue. To some extent, the legislative directives just noted may restrict the flexibility of the "employer" and unions. The New Hampshire Act, for example, requires all "cost items and terms and conditions of employment affecting state employees generally" to be negotiated with the negotiating committee created by the law. While one would assume that noncost, nonuniform items would be bargained separately at the unit level, the Act goes on to provide that "Negotiations regarding terms and conditions of employment unique to individual bargaining units shall be negotiated individually with the representatives of those units *by the state negotiating committee*[94] [emphasis added]." This will potentially erode the ability of local campus administrators to arrive at settlements with local faculty units unless the central committee, of necessity removed from a day-to-day acquaintance with campus problems, agrees to permit it to do so.

[92]*Mont. Rev. Codes Ann.* § 59-1609 (1975 Cum. Supp.).

[93]*N.H. Rev. Stat. Ann.* § 273-A:9 (1975).

[94]*Id.*

The second and far more significant problem that these provisions fail to address is that of whipsawing or leapfrogging by individual unions, each representing their separate bargaining units and each having access to the central employer whether or not expressly identified in the Act. This issue is not unknown in the private sector; even where a union is selected on a plant-by-plant basis the parties may agree to negotiate on a companywide basis and, where several unions are involved, they may agree to negotiate both centrally and jointly. However, the NLRB has taken the view, judicially approved, that such arrangements are wholly consensual; that is, a demand for joint or coalition bargaining is not a mandatory bargaining subject.[95]

Several states do address the question of bargaining structure directly. The New Hampshire Act adopts the NLRB's approach by providing that two or more units of employees of a single public employer may be merged into a single unit with the approval of all parties.[96] The Connecticut and Pennsylvania acts merely provide that nothing in their provisions will "be deemed to prohibit multi-unit bargaining."[97] To similar effect, the Iowa Act provides that it shall not be construed to prohibit "cooperation and coordination of bargaining between two or more bargaining units."[98] The Minnesota Act is more detailed. It permits joint negotiations by public employers and employee representatives in similar bargaining units if they voluntarily agree so to engage.[99] It also allows the governor to direct common negotiations upon the unanimous written request of representatives of units and appointing authorities, regardless of the unit

[95]See, for example, International Longshoremen's Ass'n. v. NLRB, 277 F. 2d 681 (D.C. Cir. 1960), where the court sustained a Board finding that the union violated the act by insisting on coastwide bargaining in the face of separate port certifications but denied enforcement of the Board's cease and desist order because of the subsequent agreement of the parties on a coastwide contract. The law may, however, be changing. In Newspaper Production Co. v. NLRB 503 F. 2d 821 (5th Cir. 1974), the Board found, and the court agreed, that a union that had represented an employer's craft workers and then was newly certified to represent production workers could insist to impasse, and strike, over a demand that a single contract cover both groups.

[96]*N.H. Rev. Stat. Ann.* § 273-A:10 (1975).

[97]Connecticut P.A. 566, L. 1975 § 5(b), *Pa. Stat. Ann.* tit. 43, § 1101.604(4) (1976–1977 Supp.)

[98]*Iowa Code Ann.* § 20.17(7) (1976 Supp.)

[99]*Minn. Stat.* § 179.71(4) (1976 Supp.).

determination. Since joint negotiations could reduce whipsawing, it remains to be seen whether the principle of voluntarism applied in the private sector ought to apply in the public sector; that is, if the central authority deems it beneficial, why could it not be given the means to *assure* that centrally negotiated matters be bargained in joint session with it? This approach would be at variance with the law in the private sector and would require statutory clarification.

Another device employed in both the private and public sectors —the "pattern" bargain—is more informal. As Chamberlain and Kuhn observe, "The wage settlement reached within a major bargaining unit by a management and union becomes a 'key bargain,' serving as a guide for settlements in other units. . . . There is not in any strict sense the establishment of a new bargaining unit; yet clearly for those issues set by the pattern, the bargaining unit has been informally extended beyond its scope."[100] Similarly in the public sector, a wage settlement, with a civil service association representing the bulk of the State's employees, for example, may set the pattern in percentage terms for the remainder of the state's employees.[101]

In the private sector, however, the employer's duty to bargain in good faith with the representative of the appropriate unit may limit its ability to insist adamantly on the "pattern." As Clyde Summers explains:

> Confronted with multiple bargaining units, the public employer can exercise control over bargaining only by establishing some guidelines, at least as to the size of the wage package, and limiting deviations from that guideline. In practice, one negotiation and agreement will establish a pattern to which most other agreements will be required to conform, with only limited deviations. The pattern will control not only the wage package but also such work load terms as holidays, vacations, sick leave, and length of work week. Thus one union effectively bar-

[100]N. Chamberlain and J. Kuhn, *Collective Bargaining* (2d ed.) (New York: McGraw-Hill, 1965), pp. 261–262.

[101]Cf. A. Anderson, "The Structure of Public Sector Bargaining," in S. Zagoria (Ed.), *Public Workers and Public Unions* (Englewood Cliffs, N.J.: Prentice-Hall, 1972), pp. 37, 40.

gains for the size of the wage package and common work load terms. The other unions are limited largely to bargaining over how the available wage dollars are to be allocated among pensions, insurance, and take-home pay. Each union, however, retains the ability to bargain concerning the conditions that are unique or of special interest to the employees it represents.

Pattern bargaining leads to practices which run counter to legal rules developed in the private sector as to what constitutes good faith bargaining, particularly when the pattern-setting agreement is not the first one negotiated. The public employer's refusal to settle with other unions until it has settled with the pattern-setting unit would be, according to traditional notions, bad faith bargaining. When the employer makes offers to other unions, they will want assurances that, if the pattern settlement is more favorable, they will receive equal benefits. The pattern-setting union may then object that it is being required to bargain for employees not in the unit, contrary to traditional notions of good faith bargaining.[102]

Thus, the extension of pattern bargaining in public employment as a means of rationalizing the bargaining structure requires explicit statutory treatment in contradistinction to the developed law in the private sector.

Oregon has apparently taken both devices—joint bargaining and the "pattern" bargain—and legislated them as a counterpart to its acceptance of the NLRB approach to unit determination:

(1) Notwithstanding any other provision of this chapter, whenever two or more labor organizations are certified to represent state employees in like classifications, the State of Oregon and the certified labor organization shall meet jointly at reasonable times and bargain in good faith for the purpose of establishing the compensation plan and

[102]C. W. Summers, "Public Employee Bargaining: A Political Perspective," 83 *Yale L. J.* 1156, 1191–1192 (1974).

other economic benefits, and those employment relations matters which require legislative action or are the subject of Personnel Division rule-making authority. Nothing in this subsection shall prevent a labor organization which has met in such joint sessions and which represents the majority of employees in a classification from entering into an agreement with the state employer governing the compensation or other benefits of such employees when, after a reasonable time, the representatives of the majority of employees in the classification and the representative of the minority of employees in the classification have not agreed as to the provisions of a proposed agreement.

(2) This section shall not apply to any subject which affects only a single agency, institution or other subordinate unit of the state.[103]

Two features of this provision should be noted. First, the public employer is given the power to command joint bargaining; indeed the failure to achieve a settlement in joint bargaining is made a condition precedent to separate settlements. Second and closely related, after the failure of joint bargaining the public employer is given power to settle with the representative of the largest number of employees. Presumably that agreement will set the pattern; the statute fails, however, to address the question of whether the employer must nevertheless continue in good faith bargaining with the other representatives even though he or she intends adamantly to insist on the pattern bargain, that is, the question of whether unfruitful marathon bargaining sessions are still required. Moreover, it remains to be seen whether the threat of a pattern bargain is alone sufficient to persuade the parties to form a coalition; if they fail in that effort it remains further to be seen what useful purpose is served by compelling joint sessions even for a "reasonable time."

These reservations aside, the Oregon approach does point the way to achieving a satisfactory bargaining structure from the employer's perspective. We shall propose a similar statutory approach in Chapter Three. Suffice it to say here that, given these devices, a state

[103]*Ore. Rev. Stat.* § 243.696 (1975).

need not adopt the Draconian policy of all-encompassing bargaining units.

III. Scope of Bargaining

In private employment, definition of the subjects of collective bargaining—defined under the National Labor Relations Act as "wages, hours, and other terms and conditions of employment"—serves three distinct functions. First, it defines those subjects upon which the statutory duty to meet and confer in good faith operates. An employer violates the duty to bargain if he refuses to meet and discuss matters within the scope of bargaining and to embody any agreement reached within that scope in a written agreement. The duty to bargain on a given subject, of course, does not mean that any particular form of agreement need be reached, or indeed that the subject must be included in any agreement reached. An employer may bargain on the subject of contracting out, for example, but may either refuse to put any provision dealing with that subject in the agreement, or insist upon a provision specifying that there shall be no limitations on his right to contract out work. If advanced in good faith and without being purposely proposed to frustrate the reaching of an agreement, that demand does not violate the statutory obligation to bargain. In contradistinction, a subject outside the scope of the mandatory duty to bargain may be advanced by either party in the bargaining process, but the other party may, without violating the statute, simply refuse to discuss it. The words "wages, hours, and other terms and conditions of employment," then, serve to distinguish those matters on which an employer is required to bargain and those on which he may, but is not required, to do so.

Much more significant in practice is a derivative function of the definition. The duty to bargain implies a duty not to take unilateral action without first bargaining. This applies both in the absence of an agreement and during the term of an agreement. It follows that an employer may not at any time make any change on any matter within the scope of the statutory definition without first proposing the change to the bargaining representative, meeting with the representative, and seeking to achieve agreement. Unilateral action as to a mandatory subject of bargaining, even if undertaken in utmost good faith, constitutes a per se violation of the duty to bargain.[104]

[104]NLRB v. Katz, 369 U.S. 736 (1962).

Finally, the distinction between matters within and without the scope of mandatory bargaining under the National Labor Relations Act is significant in determining whether insistence to the point of impasse on a particular demand violates the Act. Although a party may propose nonmandatory matters in bargaining it may not insist to the point of impasse that the other party agree on such matters. A party may, however, put a proposal on a nonmandatory subject on the table as a bargaining chip to be traded against concessions on a mandatory subject so long as that party does not insist upon agreement on the nonmandatory subject as the sole price of an agreement.[105]

All the above refers to the distinction between *mandatory* and *permissive* subjects of bargaining. Under NLRB law a single, if sometimes uncertain, line divides the mandatory and nonmandatory subjects of bargaining without regard to the context in which the distinction is to be made. Note, however, that in all three contexts the distinction between matters within the scope of "wages, hours, and other terms and conditions of employment" and those outside of that area is unrelated to the legality and enforceability of any agreement made. The matter of pensions for persons already retired, for example, is not within the scope of mandatory bargaining, since the beneficiaries of any such bargain are not employees and are therefore not within the constituency that the union is authorized to represent in collective bargaining.[106] Nevertheless, an agreement between an employer and a union providing for increased pensions for retired employees would be, absent any other impediment, entirely permissible and enforceable. That the subject is not a mandatory subject of bargaining is significant only in that an employer can, without violating his statutory duty, refuse to discuss the matter with the union or unilaterally increase (or decrease) the pensions of those already retired without first bargaining with the union, and also in that a union's insistence to the point of impasse on a change as the price for an agreement would constitute a refusal to bargain.

In practice, the distinction between the mandatory and permissive is least significant in the context of its most direct application. It

---

[105]Oil, Chemical and Atomic Workers, Local 3-89 v. NLRB, 405 F. 2d 1111 (1968).
[106]Allied Chemical & Alkali Workers v. Pittsburgh Plate Glass Co., 401 U.S. 907 (1971).

does not much matter, in private industrial employment, whether or not an employer who is determined not to increase the pensions of retired employees agrees to discuss the matter with the union before saying no. Since the duty to bargain implies no duty to agree, the careful definition of what must be discussed on request and what can be simply ignored with a "no comment" serves little useful purpose. The distinction has more practical meaning in the context of the prohibition on insistence to impasse. Even in this context, however, its significance is limited by the doctrine that a permissive subject may be joined with a mandatory subject as part of a package so long as an alternative package consisting solely of mandatory matters is offered as an alternative. An employer anxious to change an existing and unexpired benefit agreement, for example (a purely permissive subject if not contractually open to negotiations) can, without violating the duty to bargain, offer a substantially higher wage settlement, contingent upon union agreement to the change, so long as he also offers a lower wage settlement without the change.[107]

This is not to say that there are not cases in which the mandatory-permissive distinction has some significance in these contexts. Most of them, however, derive their importance from circumstances quite apart from any desire to compel an employer (or a union) to bargain about a subject. When a strike is lost (or an employer locks out), the rights of the strikers (or the locked-out employees) may depend in significant degree on whether there was an antecedent unfair labor practice. Substantial rights, therefore, may turn on whether the prior refusal to discuss a particular subject or the insistence on a particular point constituted a refusal to bargain in violation of the statute.

It is in the unilateral action context that the distinction achieves direct practical significance. And, indeed, the great bulk of the litigation on the subject has arisen because of unilateral action taken by employers.[108] *Inland Steel*, which established that pensions were a mandatory subject of bargaining, was a unilateral action case. So was *Pittsburgh Plate Glass*,[109] which established that pensions for those

[107]See Oil, Chemical & Atomic Workers, Local 3-89 v. NLRB, note 105 *supra*.

[108]Inland Steel Co. v. NLRB, 170 F. 2d 247 (7th Cir. 1948).

[109]Allied Chemical & Alkali Workers v. Pittsburgh Plate Glass Co., 404 U.S. 157 (1971).

already retired, were not. *Fibreboard*, the most frequently discussed case, and the one that has supplied most of the foundation for an expansive interpretation of the mandatory classification,[110] was a unilateral action case. The union that prosecuted that case did not complain that the Fibreboard Company refused to discuss a proposed limit on contracting out at the bargaining table; it complained, rather, that Fibreboard had contracted out the work of its members without first offering to bargain with the union about the matter.

Even in this context, however, the distinction is principally significant only insofar as it is not fully understood. Once it is appreciated that contracting out is, indeed, a mandatory subject of bargaining, any employer desirous of doing precisely what Fibreboard did can still do so. It is necessary only to talk to the union first or, if advance carte blanche is desired, to insist to the point of impasse on a contractual provision that it has the right to contract work out. It is extremely doubtful that the *Fibreboard* decision had any substantial effect on the actual practice of contracting out. Similarly, it is entirely clear that the decision in *Pittsburgh Plate Glass*—that pensions for those already retired is not a mandatory subject of bargaining—has not diminished in the least the incidence of collective agreements providing for increases in such pensions.

None of the foregoing has any application to a quite different distinction under the National Labor Relations Act, one that has no relationship to the words "wages, hours, and terms and conditions of employment." This is the distinction between the permitted and the forbidden. Certain agreements, although they are within the statutory language, are simply forbidden. An agreement that only union members be hired, for example, or one that says that no employee shall be required to work on nonunion goods, is unlawful, although clearly concerned with the terms and conditions of employment. There is, obviously, no duty to bargain about such agreements, and, indeed, any use of economic pressure to obtain them is itself an unfair labor practice. More importantly, an agreement on a prohibited subject is unenforceable and void. This distinction, unlike the mandatory-permissive distinction, has a direct and meaningful

[110]Fibreboard Paper Products Corp. v. NLRB, 379 U.S. 203 (1964).

impact not only on the bargaining process but on the employment relationship with which the bargaining is concerned.

In the public sector, the difference between the mandatory-permissive distinction and the permitted-prohibited distinction has sometimes been hopelessly confused. The analysis is beclouded by notions of sovereignty and the related prohibition of the delegation of public power to private groups.[111] Apart from these doctrinal arguments, it has been asserted that the special features of public employment mandate a scope of bargaining narrower than in the private sector.[112] Unlike the private sector, decision-making in the public sector is political; the issues to be decided are of moment, though to considerably varying degree, to the body politic. From this it is argued that the substitution of bilateral bargaining between organized public employees and representatives of the public employer for the "normal" political process will freeze other interest groups out of the decision-making process and thus "distort" the political process. The distortion will, it is suggested, yield relatively greater power to public sector unions than to their private sector counterparts because the fragmented character of political decision-making makes a monolithic union relatively stronger, particularly if it compels bargaining concessions by threatening a strike. Moreover, some have been concerned that the rigidities imposed by a collective agreement may hinder the public employer's ability to act or react in the public interest. They would therefore narrow the area for negotiation in order to limit the ambit of future inflexibility.

To be sure, these arguments have not gone unchallenged.[113]

---

[111]See generally J. Weitzman, *The Scope of Bargaining in Public Employment* (New York: Praeger, 1975).

[112]See generally H. Wellington and R. Winter, *The Unions and the Cities* (Washington, D.C.: Brookings Institution, 1972); J. H. Leddy, "Negotiating with School Teachers: Anatomy of a Muddle," 33 *Ohio St. L. Rev.* 811 (1972); R. E. Doherty, "The Politics of Public Sector Unionism," 81 *Yale L. J.* 758 (1972); S. R. Goldstein, "Book Commentary: *The Unions and the Cities*," 22 *Buff. L. Rev.* 603 (1973).

[113]See generally C. W. Summers, "Public Employee Bargaining: A Political Perspective," 83 *Yale L. J.* 1156 (1974). See also L. B. Kaden, "The Potential of Collective Bargaining in Public Employment," 81 *Yale L. J.* 772 (1972); D. H. Wollett, "The Bargaining Process in the Public Sector: What Is Bargainable?" 51 *Ore. L. Rev.* 177 (1971); R. E. Doherty and W. E. Oberer, *Teachers, School Boards and Collective Bargaining: A Changing of the Guard* (New York: School of Industrial Relations, 1967).

Nevertheless, there is considerable support for a narrowed scope of bargaining in the public sector. This has had several significant consequences. First, in deciding whether a particular issue is a "term and condition of employment" under a state statute that tracks the federal language, many labor boards and courts have tended to use a balancing test to determine whether the disputed matter primarily affects individual employee interests or impinges on agency policy-making. The difficulty in distinguishing these overlapping areas was pointed out by the Kansas Supreme Court in construing the statute applicable to the state's schoolteachers: "It does little good, we think, to speak of negotiability in terms of 'policy' versus something that is not 'policy.' Salaries are a matter of policy, and so are vacations and sick leaves. Yet we cannot doubt the authority of the [school] board to negotiate and bind itself on these questions."[114] Nevertheless, it too adopted a balancing of personal interest against policy-making. "The key, as we see it, is how direct the impact of an issue is on the well-being of the individual teacher, as opposed to its effect on the operation of the school system as a whole."[115] This general approach has been followed widely.[116]

Second, several states have chosen to enumerate their "management rights" as a specific statutory counterweight to granting public employee bargaining rights over terms and conditions of employment, although some commit such "policy" matters to "meet-and-confer," but nonbargaining, status. While in the private sector such "managerial prerogatives" would be viewed as permissive but legal subjects for bargaining, the theories advanced for their exemption in the public sector, regardless of whether management rights are explicitly outlined in the statute, logically require such matters to be viewed as subjects upon which any agreement would be prohibited.

[114]Nat'l Educ. Ass'n of Shawnee Mission, Inc. v. Board of Educ., 512 P. 2d 426, 435 (Kan. 1973).

[115]*Id.*

[116]School Dist. of Seward Educ. Ass'n v. School Dist. of Seward, 118 Neb. 722, 199 N.W. 2d 752 (1972); Aberdeen Educ. Ass'n v. Board of Educ., 215 N.W. 2d 837 (S.D. 1974); City of Biddeford v. Biddeford Teachers Ass'n, 304 A. 2d 387 (Me. 1973); Joint School Dist. No. 8 v. WERC, 37 Wis. 2d 483, 155 N.W. 2d 78 (1967); West Hartford Educ. Ass'n v. DeCourcy, 162 Conn. 566, 295 A. 2d 526 (1972). Most recently see City of Beloit v. WERC 92 LRRM 3318 (Wis. Sup. Ct. June 2, 1976).

The Hawaii Act, for example, makes this quite explicit by forbidding the parties to agree to any proposal interfering with the enumerated rights of the public employer,[117] as do the Kansas[118] and Iowa[119] acts.

Relatedly, matters that the parties may wish to bargain about may also be a subject of state legislation or regulation. Several statutes address the relationship of the collective agreement to other state laws and one nagging problem is that another state law may be the enactment creating and giving broad managerial power to the employing state agency. The Pennsylvania Act, for example, makes provision for both cases. The first merely provides that the parties may not be required to bargain over matters of inherent managerial policy;[120] thus it seems to make them legal but permissive subjects. The second, however, forbids the parties from implementing any provision "in violation of, or inconsistent with, or in conflict with"[121] any state law. This raises the problem of reconciling bargaining rights with the broad statutory grant of power to the employing agency to manage the enterprise. The Pennsylvania Supreme Court, following a New York precedent, concluded that only if state law mandates that a particular responsibility be discharged by the public employer alone will bargaining on it be precluded, even if it otherwise has an impact on matters falling properly within the scope of bargaining.[122]

In sum, the arguments for a narrowed scope of bargaining in the public sector imply that matters of basic agency policy or inherent managerial prerogative be viewed not as permissive but as prohibited subjects. As a result, considerable ambiguity has surrounded not the duty but the power of the parties to bargain. Moreover, this ambiguity

[117]*Hawaii Rev. Stat.* § 89-9(d) (1975).

[118]*Kan. Stat. Ann.* § 75-4330(a) (1975 Supp.).

[119]*Iowa Code Ann.* § 20.17(6) (1976 Supp.).

[120]*Pa. Stat. Ann.* tit. 43, § 1101.702 (1976–1977 Supp.).

[121]*Id.* § 1101.703.

[122]PLRB v. State College Area School Dist., 337 A. 2d 262 (Pa. 1975). For a review of the situation in Pennsylvania see J. J. Loewenberg and J. W. Klinger, "Scope of Bargaining in the Public Sector: The Pennsylvania Experience"; paper presented at the George Taylor Memorial Conference at Temple University (Sept. 1975). So, for example, it appears that public employers can agree to arbitrate employee terminations. Board of Educ. v. Philadelphia Federation of Teachers, 346 A. 2d 35 (Pa. 1975). Cf. Lincoln University v. Lincoln University Chapter, AAUP, 354 A. 2d 576 (Pa. 1976).

is not solely the result of an enumeration of management rights in the statute or a prohibition on agreement in conflict with other statutes. The New York Act, for example, contains neither (save for a prohibition on bargaining on retirement benefits), and the New York Court of Appeals has approved the state PERB's adoption of the mandatory-permissive distinction.[123] Nevertheless, the court has implied that the ability to bargain may be limited by "plain and clear"[124] prohibitions in the statute or decisional law and more recently observed that "the freedom to contract in exclusively private enterprises or matters does not blanket public school matters because of the governmental interests and public concerns which may be involved. . . ."[125] Thus even while sustaining the enforceability of an agreement on the permissive subject of a "no lay-off" clause, the court kept open the possibility that other such provisions might not be enforceable.[126] Similarly, the Supreme Judicial Court of Massachusetts recently concluded, despite an amendment to the state's collective bargaining law expressly allowing the collective agreement to prevail over conflicting rules, regulations, or statutes on matters within the scope of bargaining, that a school board nevertheless lacked the power to agree not to

---

[123]West Irondequoit Teachers Ass'n v. Helsby, 35 N.Y. 2d 46, 358 NYS 2d 720, 315 N.E. 2d 775 (1974). For a very thorough review of New York law as of 1975, see generally R. D. Helsby, "Scope of Bargaining under New York State's Taylor Law"; paper presented at the George Taylor Memorial Conference at Temple University (Sept. 1975).

[124]Syracuse Teachers Ass'n v. Bd. of Educ., 35 NY 2d 743, 320 N.E. 2d 646 (1974). This has been viewed as a retreat from the verbal test adopted in Board of Educ. v. Associated Teachers of Huntington, 30 NY 2d 122, 282 N.E. 2d 109, 331 NYS 2d 17 (1972), relied on by the Pennsylvania Supreme Court. See generally R. F. Kortez and R. J. Rabin, "1975 Survey of New York Law—Labor Relations Law," 27 *Syr. L. Rev.* 139 (1976).

[125]Susquehanna Valley School Dist. v. Susquehanna Valley Teachers Ass'n, 37 NY 2d 614, 339 N.E. 2d 132, 133–134 (1975).

[126]Board of Educ. v. Yonkers Federation of Teachers 92 LRRM 3328, 3330–3331 (N.Y. Ct. App., July 1, 1976): "This is not to say, however, that all job security clauses are valid and enforceable or that they are valid and enforceable under all circumstances. Notably, the job security clause involved in this case and the staff size clause in [another] case were of relatively brief duration, three years and two years respectively. Nor were the clauses negotiated at a time of financial emergency between parties of unequal bargaining power. Most important, the job security clause in the instant case is explicit in its protection of the teachers from abolition of their positions due to budgetary stringencies. . . ." See also Burke v. Bowen, 92 LRRM 3331 (N.Y. Ct. App., July 1, 1976).

abolish a position during the term of the collective agreement.[127] However, the Oregon Court of Appeals has taken a different approach.[128]

Finally, the context in which disputes over the scope of bargaining arise in the public sector often differs from the private sector. We have noted that private sector charges of an illegal refusal to bargain are filed most often after a unilateral act of the employer or in the context of a strike. In the former case the union attempts to avail itself of the employer's failure to have consulted the union to secure redress from the labor board for the affected employees. In the latter the union seeks to have the strike viewed as one occasioned by the employer's unfair labor practice, thereby affording greater protection for the striking employees than they would have if they engaged simply in an economic contest. In neither case can it be said that the union's real motivation is actually to obtain bargaining about the particular issue. While unilateral action has produced disputes over the scope of bargaining in the public sector, very often the determination of the issue is sought either by a charge filed during bargaining, that is, almost as an advisory opinion from the labor board about what the parties may bargain about, or by a challenge to a contractual provision after it has been agreed to. In these instances the union's interest may actually be in bargaining (or protecting the bargain struck) rather than in the ancillary effects of an improper refusal to bargain. This suggests that in the public sector—far more than in the private sector—the scope of bargaining question actually concerns what the parties may bargain about.

The interplay of these various distinctions is well illustrated in New Jersey, whose labor board, until recently, lacked power over

---

[127]School Committee of Hanover v. Curry, 343 N.E. 2d 144 (Mass. 1976), School Committee of Braintree v. Raymond, 343 N.E. 2d 145 (Mass. 1976).

[128]In Springfield Educ. Ass'n v. Springfield School Dist., 547 P. 2d 647 (Ore. App. 1976) the court rejected the state PERB's determination that policy matters within the exclusive jurisdiction of the school board were forbidden subjects. It held them to be permissive subjects in applying the balancing test so widely applied elsewhere. However, the court also held that rules on student discipline promulgated by the state board of education would set a standard to which collective agreements on that point would have to adhere. Sutherlin Educ. Ass'n v. Sutherlin School Dist., 92 LRRM 2963 (Ore. App.) (Apr. 12, 1976).

unfair labor practices and whose courts were compelled to consider several cases in higher education dealing with the scope of bargaining. The New Jersey law provides for bargaining on wages, hours, and terms, and conditions of employment but, while not providing a management rights exemption, did provide that the collective bargaining law shall not modify or annul any other state statute. The New Jersey Supreme Court applied that clause in determining that the academic calendar of a community college is reserved to the board of trustees under its general grant of managerial authority by state law and is thus not a subject of mandatory bargaining. The court concluded that the board of trustees had negotiated

> on the matters directly and intimately affecting the faculty's working terms and conditions, such as compensation, hours, work loads, sick leaves, personal and sabbatical leaves, physical accommodations, grievance procedures, etc. It declined to negotiate the major educational policy of the calendar though it did make provision in its governance structure for a calendar committee with student, faculty and administration representatives. While, in the interests of sound labor relations, it might well have also discussed the subject with officially designated representatives of the Association, it was under no legal mandate to do so.[129]

In essence, the court adhered to the verbal distinction between "major educational policy" and "terms and conditions of employment" that was viewed as unhelpful but applied nonetheless by the Kansas court. It seems that the college calendar, determining the number of days to be worked, is both a matter of educational policy and a term of employment and that coupling a balancing test with a vague verbal formula creates considerable uncertainty about what is mandatorily bargainable.

Shortly thereafter, an appeals court was confronted with determining the negotiability of the student-faculty ratio formulas

[129]Burlington County Faculty Ass'n v. Board of Trustees, 64 N.J. 10, 311 A. 2d 733, 735 (1973).

adopted by the board of higher education without bargaining with the faculty representative of Rutgers University. As the court presents it, the formulas would affect the total dollar amount requested by the board of higher education for Rutgers, although the university could negotiate further with the faculty on the distribution of the funds ultimately appropriated. Again, the court relied on the provision accommodating other state statutes and concluded that the formulas adopted by the board of higher education were nonnegotiable. The court was seemingly most persuaded by the impact negotiations would have on other interest groups.

> The Board's right to make a budget recommendation for Rutgers was intended by the Legislature to be exercised freely, and in a manner that would enable it to receive an independent and analytical assessment of the budgetary needs of the University. As respondents point out, if the Employer-Employee Relations Act were construed to compel collective negotiations on the budget recommendations given to the Legislature by the Board, this obvious legislative intent would be frustrated, for the recommendations it made each year would reflect compromise and not the Board's independent judgment. As we have remarked earlier in this opinion, any member of a public or private interest group may examine any budget recommendation made by the Board and, if so minded, submit his views and appropriate data with regard thereto to the executive and legislative branches of government. This, and not collective negotiation, is the proper avenue for interested parties to follow.[130]

The issue presents, in more refined form than the college-calendar case, the dilemma of the "policy-employment condition" dichotomy. If the formulas adopted by the board of higher education actually determined the teacher-student ratio at Rutgers (and there was evidence that it did)[131] then it was in practical effect a unilateral

---

[130]Rutgers Council AAUP v. New Jersey Board of Higher Education, 126 N.J. Super. 53, 312 A. 2d 677, 684 (App. Div. 1973).

[131]*Id.*, Appendix of Plaintiff-Appellant at 10-1 to 10-4 (correspondence be-

workload alteration, which was mandatorily bargainable in the item-
ized list of bargainable subjects set out by the court in the community
college calendar case. Thus the court proceeds on the assumption, as
it must, that the formula was merely an analytical device employed by
the board to assess the Rutgers budget request. On the other hand, the
largest sum in any institutional budget goes for instructional costs,
essentially faculty salaries, which the collective bargaining law subjects to the process of negotiation. Thus, the Act requires that at least
insofar as those budget items are concerned the governor's request to
the legislature is intended precisely to "reflect compromise" or at
least an effort to reach agreement beforehand. Since that request is
subject to legislative approval no interest group is foreclosed from
access to the final authority to examine or comment on the submission. The case might have been easier for the court had the Rutgers
faculty bargained with the board of higher education rather than with
its own administration for nowhere does the court address the board's
action as that of a public employer rather than that of a remote "neu-
tral" administrative agency.

Similarly the New Jersey Supreme Court considered whether
the state's board of higher education breached its duty to bargain by
unilaterally adopting guidelines for the acquisition of tenure in the
state college system.[132] Because of its concern about the eventual
"tenuring-in" of the state college faculties the board adopted a series
of resolutions without prior negotiation with the faculty's collective
bargaining agent. The board required each state college to achieve a
"reasonable proportion" of tenured faculty over a ten-year period;
each would be required either to "impose specific restrictions" (conceivably in the form of numerical quotas) or develop more rigorous
review procedures for conferring tenure. In addition, tenured faculty
were to be reevaluated at least once every five years. The court found
the board had not breached its duty to bargain, but had merely pro-
nounced "major educational policy" within its expertise. It relied on
the "reasonable" nature of the guidelines themselves as well as on the
recommendation of the national tenure commission. Thus the

---

tween President Bloustein and Dean Young on class loads and ratios).

[132]Association of New Jersey State College Faculties, Inc. v. Dunegan, 64 N.J. 338, 316
A. 2d 425 (1927).

opportunity for job retention by a bargaining unit member may, by the court's conclusion, be limited unilaterally by the public employer even by the adoption of a numerical quota, without the policy or its consequences being first subjected to the mediating influence of negotiations with the faculty's representative. The court ignored the fact that, while bargaining in good faith, the public employer might nevertheless have insisted on the proposal and that the board could have implemented it in the event agreement was not reached. Exempting the matter from the scope of bargaining denied the faculty the chance to have bargained about a policy clearly affecting terms and conditions of employment.

The New Jersey legislature recently repealed the language that had served as one of the statutory buttresses for these decisions. The provision now prohibits the collective bargaining law solely from modifying any state pension statute.[133] The New Jersey Supreme Court has held that guidelines on outside employment for state college faculty adopted unilaterally by the board of higher education were mandatorily bargainable.[134] The decision was based on prior decisional law, and the court declined to apply the now-modified language of the accommodations clause; the guidelines were deemed to affect directly the work and welfare of college employees and not a major educational policy. Thus the court now seems to have made plain that its prior construction of the statute depended only slightly, if at all, on the language of the accommodations clause. Indeed a recent construction of the Act by an intermediate appellate court subsequent to the amendment indicates at least in dictum that matters of basic educational policy continue to remain exclusively with the school board and are forbidden bargaining subjects.[135]

However, the New Jersey Public Employment Relations Commission (PERC), which has been given power to decide unfair labor practices, has opined that basic managerial prerogatives in higher education are permissive subjects of bargaining. So, for example, the

[133]*N.J. Stat. Ann.* § 13:13A 8.1 (1976 Supp.), amended by L. 1974, c. 163, § 6.

[134]Association of New Jersey State College Faculties, Inc. v. New Jersey Board of Higher Educ., 66 N.J. 72, 328 A. 2d 235 (1974).

[135]Board of Education of North Bergen v. North Bergen Federation of Teachers, 92 LRRM 2826 (N.J. Super., App. Div.) (April 27, 1976). *See also* Red Bank Educ. Ass'n v. Warrington, 351 A. 2d 778 (N.J. Super., App. Div.) (1976).

demand by the Rutgers AAUP that no examinations be scheduled on Saturdays or Sundays was held by the New Jersey PERC to be a basic educational management decision that the administration could refuse to talk about, that is, it was a permissive subject.[136] However, the Commission held that the *impact* of the decision as it affects conditions of employment was a mandatory subject. Thus the faculty agent could properly require the university to bargain about whether unit members may be required to proctor examinations on Saturdays and Sundays or whether they are to be paid for such activity; that is, while the practical result may well be the same, the form of the bargaining proposal determined whether it was mandatory or permissive. The distinction means that the selection of the wrong formulation for the proposal would presumably permit the administration simply to refuse to discuss the issue entirely.

The foregoing brief review has led us to the following observations. First, while the determination that a particular matter is a mandatory bargaining subject in the public sector will, as in the private sector, prohibit unilateral employer action, a contrary determination may have the effect of prohibiting an agreement altogether; thus any such determination in the public sector potentially has a far greater impact on what the parties bargain about than it has in the private sector. Second, the mandatory-permissive distinction is employed in the private sector in part to narrow the permissible area of an economic contest; thus to the extent alternative means of dispute-resolution are employed in the public sector the distinction may want a sound justification.[137] Indeed even in private sector negotiations, a party with sufficient bargaining strength can secure agreement on a nonmandatory item without impermissibly insisting to impasse; this places in question whether the distinction is useful at all outside the context of unilateral action. Third, the dichotomy between major educational policy and working conditions, whether employed to distinguish the forbidden from the permissive or the permissive from the mandatory is often so fine as to be almost ineffable. Accordingly,

[136]Rutgers, The State University v. Rutgers Council, AAUP, N.J. P.E.R.C. No. 76-13 (1976).

[137]Cf. H.T. Edwards, "The Emerging Duty to Bargain in the Public Sector," 71 *Mich. L. Rev.* 885, 922-923 (1973).

the question remains whether the definition of the scope of bargaining can accommodate the various contexts in which disputes over it arise while remaining responsive to the needs of both administrations and of faculties in institutions of higher education. We shall propose a solution in Chapter Three. As a preface, however, we should turn more explicitly to that feature of higher education that has been the touchstone of our analysis, namely, the system of academic government, and explain the special impact the scope of bargaining definition has on it.

Bargaining and Academic Governance

As we stressed at the outset, faculties perform work that cursory view would take as being of a managerial character: They formulate basic educational policies and play a primary if not dispositive role on matters of personnel selection and retention. The system of academic government rests on the institution's need to secure professional judgment and to assure faculty morale by providing for its participation. Neither of these reasons are inconsistent with collective bargaining. The available evidence suggests that faculties resort to collective bargaining in part to protect or advance their role in institutional decisions; one recent study asserts that significant increases in faculty participation have been produced by collective bargaining at institutions that lacked a strong tradition of academic government.[138]

However, if matters of governance are mandatorily bargainable, then the principle of exclusive representation requires, at least at first blush, that the administration deal solely with the union on such matters. Related to this principle is the perhaps considerable overlap between educational policy matters, for which the traditional internal faculty organs may have primary jurisdiction, and terms and conditions of employment, for which the union has exclusive jurisdiction. The basic problem, then, lies in reconciling the faculty union's role qua union with the faculty's role qua faculty.

One alternative is to exempt matters of governance from the scope of mandatory bargaining. Support for this approach can be found in the private and, to a greater extent, the public sector. The NLRB almost confronted the issue when the administration of St.

---

[138]F. Kemerer and J. Baldridge, *Unions on Campus* (San Francisco: Jossey-Bass, 1975).

John's University (New York) charged that the faculty bargaining agent had insisted to impasse on four nonmandatory demands: (1) the incorporation of the 1966 Statement on Government of Colleges and Universities in the collective agreement; (2) faculty representation on the university's board of trustees; (3) a statement of administration responsibilities, including a declaration that the university administration should function in an atmosphere of collegiality; and (4) seemingly toward the goal envisioned by (3), a procedure for the selection of the university's president and deans that would require faculty participation and evaluation.

The NLRB's regional director dismissed the charge, having found that the bargaining agent had not insisted to impasse.[139] Nevertheless, he opined by letter that the demands were not mandatorily bargainable. While his opinion is not precedential it was sufficiently influential for the agency's general counsel to adopt in his quarterly report.[140] The regional director's letter, as thus approved by the Board's general counsel, represents the position of the agency's independent prosecutorial division, and the theory embraced by it will doubtless be presented eventually for Board disposition.

Both opinions treated all the demands as a single entity and adduced three interrelated reasons for concluding them to be not mandatorily bargainable: (1) they relate to the selection of supervisory personnel by the employer and thus do not concern the terms and conditions of employment of unit members; (2) they relate to the selection of individuals who may act as managerial representatives for collective bargaining or for grievance adjustment and thus fall afoul of the National Labor Relation Act's section 8(b)(1)(B), which prohibits union coercion or restraint of an employer in the selection of his representatives for those purposes; and (3) a conflict of interest is created by the participation of bargaining unit employees in the selection of managerial employees.

The second argument does present a troublesome obstacle to bargaining proposals concerning faculty participation in the selec-

[139]Letter from Samuel M. Kaynard, Regional Director for Region 29 NLRB to St. John's University Re: 29-CB-1858 (Feb. 19, 1975).

[140]*1975 Labor Relations Yearbook* (Washington, D.C.: Bureau of National Affairs, 1976), pp. 273–275.

tion of higher administrators. However, the legislative history of section 8(b)(1)(B) indicates a technical goal wholly unconcerned with the role of faculty in the life of the institution.[141] Suffice it to say here that no state collective bargaining law has incorporated this highly specialized provision of the Act.

The remainder of the rationale is based on an assumption that the Act requires a clear distinction between management and employee and that any union efforts to blur the distinction is an intrusion into management prerogative and thus not mandatorily bargainable.

> Faculty participation in the selection of these managerial representatives would necessarily affect the ultimate choice of representatives and the attitude of those chosen once they took office. Thus, there might be mixed loyalties of those selected, with obligations running not only to the institution but also to the faculty to which they would be indebted for their appointments.[142]

This reasoning is deficient in several regards. First, it ignores entirely the body of Board unit decisions that struggle to apply the Act's dichotomy between labor and management to university life where the faculty itself possesses seemingly "managerial" authority and where deans (and even presidents) are viewed as academic leaders responsible to the faculty as well as managers responsible to the governing board. Indeed Member Fanning had pointed out that if the Board was to rely on the faculty's role in institutional governance as a factor in shaping the unit, the Board must assume that such participation constitutes a mandatory bargaining subject.[143] Second, the conclusion is built on the assumption that deans will not be able to function if selected or evaluated by faculty. Thus it ignores the prevalence of faculty participation in decanal selection and evaluation

---

[141]The primary purpose of the provision was to prevent unions from trying to force employers into or out of multi-employer bargaining units. See generally Florida Power & Light Co. v. IBEW, 417 U.S. 790 (1974).

[142]Letter of the Regional Director, *supra* note 139 at 3.

[143]New York University, 205 NLRB No. 16 (1973) (Member Fanning dissenting in part).

both within and outside collective bargaining. Finally, while each of the four demands requires separate attention, the regional director and the general counsel chose to treat them as being all of a piece, indeed, in the latter case, of presenting the far more general question of the negotiability of "collegiality." For example, faculty voting membership on the governing board—the second demand—is not a common academic practice either under collective bargaining or outside of it. That demand, at least, would seem to be a nonmandatory one under the federal act. The Statement on Government, however, deals with the role of the faculty in educational policy-making and personnel decisions; it had already been adopted as university policy, refined in university practice, and clearly concerned the work of unit members. Such matters are commonly bargained about, either directly or by the incorporation of a broad "past practice" clause encompassing the faculty's established role in educational and personnel decisions. Nevertheless, the Board's prosecutorial division lumped the entire matter under the heading of "collegiality" and viewed it as a permissive subject of bargaining.

The reasoning of the NLRB's general counsel has been followed in the public sector. The New York PERB has held the CUNY faculty union's demand that students be prohibited from serving on faculty personnel committees to be a nonmandatory subject.[144] The PERB stated that although evaluation *procedures* were negotiable, the *composition* of evaluation committees under those procedures was a management prerogative. In response to Member Crowley's dissenting opinion that such a distinction was anomalous where intraunit peer evaluation is involved, the two member majority went to some length to state its support for faculty participation in academic decision-making.

> The right of the faculty to negotiate over terms and conditions of employment does not enlarge or contract the traditional prerogatives of collegiality; neither does it subsume them. These prerogatives may continue to be exercised through the traditional channels of academic committees

[144]Board of Higher Education of the City of New York, PERB No. U-0904 (April 29, 1974) (slip opinion).

and faculty senates and may be altered in the same manner as was available prior to the enactment of the Taylor Law. We note with approval the observation that "faculty must continue to manage, even if that is an anomaly. They will, in a sense, be on both sides of the bargaining table." We would qualify this observation, however; faculty may be on both sides of the table, but not their union.[145]

The Board concluded that collective bargaining "is not designed to resolve policy questions regarding the structure of governance," inasmuch as other interest groups may be disabled from participation in that decision by bilateral agreement.

Similarly the New Jersey PERC considered several bargaining proposals trenching on academic government at Rutgers University to be permissive subjects.[146] One, for example, would have required faculty participation on promotion review committees theretofore entirely administrative. The Commission distinguished the subject (promotion) from the demand (composition of the review committee) and explained that, "The University cannot be required to negotiate the composition of a body created by the University to assist the University's Board of Governors in making those decisions. This is completely up to management. If it chooses to share this function at a particular level in the decision-making process with an equal number of AAUP or faculty members, it may do so. However, it is not required to negotiate regarding such matters."[147] As in the New York PERB decision, the PERC opined that in this way the systems of collegiality and collective bargaining may continue to function harmoniously for "the university is free to continue to delegate to collegial entities whatever managerial functions it chooses."[148]

The New York and New Jersey decisions arose in the context of bargaining. The Michigan Employment Relations Commission considered a similar challenge in the context of unilateral action.[149] The

[145]*Id.* at 8.

[146]Rutgers, The State University v. Rutgers Council, AAUP, *supra* note 136.

[147]*Id.* at 13.

[148]*Id.* at 6.

[149]Central Michigan University, MERC Case No. C74A-19 (Jan. 30, 1976).

trustees of Central Michigan University adopted a policy on teaching effectiveness recommended to it by the institution's academic senate —composed of administrative, faculty, and student representatives. The Commission majority disagreed with its administrative law judge, who found the adoption to be a violation of the duty to bargain, and opined that it was merely a statement of trustee preference rather than a binding directive. Nevertheless, the majority felt it "advisable to discuss the differences between institutions of higher learning and other public employers as related to the scope of bargaining,"[150] which they stressed could be found in the fact that faculty members have a significant role in the management of their institutions. From this they concluded that the policy, produced by the established governance system, was "predominantly a matter of educational policy not mandatorily negotiable," though the impact of any such policy on terms and conditions of bargaining would be negotiable. One member dissented.

The NLRB's general counsel and the New York, New Jersey, and Michigan public employment boards have attempted to separate bargaining and governance entirely by identifying the latter as a management prerogative not mandatorily bargainable. This approach suffers from several serious infirmities. While attempting to preserve the governance system by insulating it from bargaining, this approach actually places the governance system at the discretion of the institution's governing board. At a minimum it allows the employer to take unilateral action concerning the governance system at any time save insofar as it might first be compelled to bargain about the "impact" of its decision on working conditions. Moreover, if in the public sector matters of such "major educational policy" are ultimately held in the jurisdiction to be forbidden rather than permissive subjects, the exemption of governance would allow a governing board to eviscerate the system entirely; it would, for example, prohibit the agent from securing the faculty's already established role even through a general past-practices clause in the collective agreement. Assuming governance is a permissive subject, that determination is often perceived as weighting the bargaining process to hinder the bargaining agent's ability to effect a satisfactory accommodation with

150*Id.* at 15.

the governance system.[151] However, it is quite clear that the issues of "collegiality" and "working conditions" cannot be cabined as conveniently as this approach assumes. Rather than allow for a more flexible bargaining position, adoption of the mandatory-permissive approach to governance may well clog the bargaining process with undue legalism. Given the rather different context in which scope of bargaining determinations arise in the public sector, adherence to the mandatory-permissive distinction will engender litigation, during the course of bargaining, about what the parties must bargain about; and in view of the interrelatedness of governance and working conditions, decisions on scope of bargaining may ultimately rest on nothing more substantial than the precise form in which a bargaining proposal was put.

A second alternative for preserving the system of governance from erosion as a result of collective bargaining is to subject such matters to "meet-and-confer" requirements while exempting them from the scope of bargaining. Minnesota excludes from the duty to negotiate "matters of inherent managerial policy," including specifically the functions and programs of the employer and the selection and direction of personnel, but imposes an obligation to "meet and confer" with the representative of professional employees to discuss "policies and those matters relating to employment not included" in

---

[151]Note, for example, the advice of one experienced labor lawyer presented to the trade association of college attorneys:

> Many question the practical distinction between mandatory and permissive subjects of bargaining. A question that is often asked is, "Why shouldn't the administration be willing to discuss any matter at the bargaining table, irrespective of whether it is mandatorily bargainable or not?" After all, say the proponents of this view, "If there is a problem why shouldn't we work out a solution at the bargaining table?" The answer to this is that you will be losing a great advantage by not making the distinction. Proposals that cannot be insisted upon are the least likely to be adopted. Moreover, the administration has greater latitude to act regarding permissive subjects of bargaining which are not included within the agreement. Finally, once a subject is on the bargaining table, you may have difficulty removing it without a *quid pro quo*. Accordingly, I submit that a non-mandatory subject of bargaining which is proposed by the union should be objected to and not be bargained over unless it is to the present or future advantage of the institution or unless you are relatively sure that you can obtain a negotiation advantage.

H. Schwartzman, "The Administration's Approach to Collective Bargaining," 1 *J. of College & Univ. Law* 351, 360 (1974) (citations omitted).

the duty to negotiate.[152] Pennsylvania has a similar exclusion and imposes a duty to "meet and discuss" with the representatives of all employees on policy matters affecting wages, hours, and conditions of employment.[153] The Hawaii statute has essentially the same effect. While it excludes a whole range of subjects from negotiations, the statute makes any matter "affecting employee relations" subject to "consultation" with the exclusive representative.[154]

Two issues are posed in the administration of these provisions: whether the public employer must first exhaust the conference procedure before effecting a policy change and whether the conference procedure may result in a collective agreement. The Hawaii Act states explicitly that the employer is "to make every reasonable effort to consult" the bargaining agent prior to effecting any change in "any major policy affecting employment relations."[155] The Pennsylvania Act, however, triggers the consultation procedure upon the request of the bargaining agent; thus it is not entirely clear whether the public employer is required to inform the agent in advance of a proposed policy change and exhaust the discussion requirement before implementing it. Further, the Hawaii Act makes it abundantly clear that any agreement is forbidden that would interfere with the rights of a public employer to direct employees, to determine their qualifications and standards for work, or to determine the means and personnel by which the employer's operations are to be conducted. The Pennsylvania Act provides to similar effect that any decisions made as a result of the discussion procedure remain with the public employer and be final; thus it appears that a collective agreement is not contemplated. The Minnesota Act is silent in both regards.

As a means of reconciling bargaining and governance the "meet and confer" (or "discuss" or "consult") approach presents significant difficulties. The intent of these provisions is to allow employees to participate in the formulation of agency policy but not as a subject of collective bargaining. However, the distinction between "meet and confer" and bargaining is not self-evident, since the duty to bargain is

[152]*Minn. Stat.* § 179.66(1), (3) (1976 Supp.).

[153]*Pa. Stat. Ann.* tit. 43 § 1101.702 (1976–1977 Supp.).

[154]*Hawaii Rev. Stat.* § 89-9(c) (1975 Supp.).

[155]*Id.*

usually defined in language comparable to that of the National Labor Relations Act, as a duty "to meet at reasonable times and confer in good faith." These provisions thus appear to impose a duty comparable to the duty to bargain but subject to the qualification that the bargaining not result in a binding agreement. As such, these statutes appear at the same time to limit strictly the area upon which the public employer may make an agreement while imposing upon it a duty not to take unilateral action virtually identical to that derived from the duty to bargain, but over a greatly expanded area. Thus, the employer's freedom of unilateral action may be more severely restricted than it would be were such policy matters considered merely permissive bargaining subjects.[156] On the other hand, inasmuch as agreement is forbidden, even if the employer accepts the representative's position on a particular policy matter, it is nevertheless permitted to alter that understanding at any time, subject only to the exhaustion of the consultative procedure. As a number of recent cases indicate, this may lead to litigation as to whether the "meet and confer" conferences were properly conducted that is quite comparable to litigation as to whether there has been bargaining in good faith.[157] Apart from the inevitable procedural elaboration produced by this litigation and the perhaps unnecessarily severe limitation on the employer's freedom of unilateral action, the most troublesome feature of this approach in the faculty setting is that by prohibiting agreement on governance procedures it prevents even the preservation of existing governance practices.

A third alternative for preserving academic governance is to legislate on the problem directly. For example, Montana's short-lived experiment in a separate higher education collective bargaining law provided: "Nothing in this act shall be construed as interfering with the right of the faculty senate or similar representative body of faculty, or the committees thereof from consulting with and advising any unit administration concerning matters of policy."[158]

[156]See Lipow v. Regents of the University of California, 54 Cal. App. 3d 215, 91 LRRM 2864 (Jan. 1976) for the effect of a meet-and-confer requirement on the University of California. See also Firefighters v. Pleasanton, 92 LRRM 2399 (Cal. App. April 2, 1976).

[157]*Id.* See also PLRB v. APSCUF/PAHE, 355 A. 2d 853 (Pa. Cmwlth, 1976).

[158]§ 12, H.B. 1032, Mont. L. 1974.

The major difficulty with this or any similar effort is that it may prevent the parties from arriving at an acceptable accommodation of the faculty and union roles. It is doubtful that a strong, independent faculty government can be created by legislative fiat. Moreover, the language can be read as allowing the administration to circumvent the bargaining agent by dealing directly with possibly unrepresentative faculty groups on properly bargainable matters. A more suitable approach would be to make clear that internal faculty governing agencies are not labor organizations for bargaining purposes, and we shall make that proposal in Chapter Three. The administration would then not be forbidden by law from supporting such faculty agencies while the faculty's role might nevertheless be negotiable with the faculty union.

In sum, we believe that two requirements are essential if bargaining and governance are to achieve a satisfactory accommodation with one another. First, matters of governance should be considered bargainable. We shall propose in Chapter Three an approach to public sector scope of bargaining that we believe at once accommodates both the different contexts in which disputes over it arise and the employer's need for flexibility while rejecting, at least in part, the mandatory-permissive distinction. To be sure, this holds open the possibility that the bargaining agent will limit unduly or supplant altogether independent faculty governing agencies on matters of such educational policy as curriculum. This in turn underlines the second requirement, accurately put by Joseph Garbarino: "Where competition for power and jurisdiction exist [between the union and faculty governing bodies] the primary reason is the lack of correspondence between the constituency of the senates and the membership of the bargaining unit, or, more precisely, the active membership of the union."[159]

Thus, it is of critical importance that the bargaining unit conform to the faculty governance constituency. Where the unit and governing constituency are identical it is much more likely that the two will arrive at a jurisdictional accommodation; the agent's willingness to cede jurisdiction and, conversely, its desires to assume it, may be a

[159] J. W. Garbarino, "Collegiality, Consensus, and Collective Bargaining," GERR No. 604 at F-1 (May 5, 1975).

function of the degree of consensus in the unit on the utility of the governance system as constituted. It is imperative that the two constituencies coincide so that critical academic decisions can be made by a unit uninfluenced by marginal academic or nonacademic groups.

IV. Other Provisions Accommodating Higher Education

Montana, Oregon, and, most recently, Maine have provided for student participation in the bargaining process in higher education. Oregon has further adopted a special two-stage procedure for faculty representation elections. Accordingly, examination should be made of these special provisions. In addition, it may be suggested that union security devices have particular implications for higher education and so ought to be discussed from the perspective of whether some special accommodation need be made.

Student Role in Bargaining

Three states have amended their public employee bargaining statutes by making provision for student participation in bargaining with faculty in institutions of higher education. Oregon's 1975 amendment is the most detailed.[160] It provides that the student government at any institution that has an exclusive bargaining agent representing faculty shall designate three representatives who shall (1) be allowed to attend all collective bargaining meetings, (2) be given access to all documents exchanged by the parties, including copies of any written transcripts of the bargaining sessions, (3) be allowed to comment during the bargaining sessions, and (4) be allowed to meet and confer with each of the parties prior to the execution of any agreement. The Montana amendment[161] gives similarly designated students the right to meet and confer with the parties prior to negotiations and the right to observe negotiations, but provides for participation only in the caucuses of the employer negotiating team and for the right to meet and confer with the board of regents before it executes an agreement with the faculty. The University of Maine Labor Relations Act was amended in 1976 to provide for student participation in collective

---

[160]*Ore. Rev. Stat.* § 243.778, added by L. 1975, Ch. 679, Sec. 2 (1975).

[161]*Mont. Rev. Code*, § 59-1502, as amended by L. 1975, Ch. 384, Sec. 1.

bargaining.[162] In Maine the students are appointed by the trustees. They "may meet and confer" with the faculty agent prior to collective bargaining, and "shall be allowed to meet and confer with the university bargaining team" during the course of negotiations. In other states, similar measures have been proposed either as amendments to existing laws or as portions of bills providing for bargaining for the first time. In all these instances, the proposals have been generated by intensive student lobbies.

The enacted statutes, and those proposed, have some obvious defects, not the least of which is their somewhat naive view of the nature of collective bargaining. Collective bargaining involves much more than the formal negotiations leading to a collective agreement. It is, or should be, a more or less continuous process in which matters of concern are dealt with as they arise, sometimes informally and sometimes formally. It is often a delicate process, frequently involving intermediaries with the formal full meetings of the bargaining teams serving only to ratify, or refuse ratification, of understandings worked out in private meetings. To insist that any observer has the right to sit in on every meeting, receive copies of every draft, and participate in every caucus can greatly obstruct, if not make impossible, the achievement of agreement.

These frictional costs of formal, mandatory student participation might be tolerable if there were sound reasons for it. We believe that there are no such reasons and that, indeed, direct student participation may pose a fundamental danger to the achievement of a system of collective bargaining compatible with sound principles of academic government.

The arguments supporting the enacted laws, and the efforts to obtain similar provisions in other states, have two quite different thrusts. The first is essentially economic. Inasmuch as the bargain struck may have a direct impact on costs, there is likely to be an effect on the price of the educational service, that is, tuition. Hence, the argument continues, the consumers who will bear this cost should be entitled to participate in the bargaining process.

The second argument goes essentially to academic concerns. Students, it is said, should have a role in decisions regarding academic

---

[162]26 *Maine Rev. Stat.* § 1024, sub-§ 4, as added by L. 1976.

content and structure. Since bargaining will inevitably affect such matters, students should be given the right to participate in the bargaining process: If, for example, the evaluation of teaching ability is to be one of the subjects of collective bargaining, the students are obviously concerned and should have a right to participate.

The first argument is, we think, spurious. As a matter of theory, assuming *arguendo* that the analogy of students to purchasers is accurate, it does not follow that the purchasers of the educational service should participate in the bargaining process. They do not in industrial bargaining. The impact on cost (and pricing) is, of course, a factor that management in the private sector considers when responding to union demands. Consumers are heard through product selection, and the impact of consumer choice depends upon the elasticity of demand for the product. If anything, students have a potentially far greater impact in the marketplace than consumers of other products. First, students are able to select the institution they attend, and the impact of tuition on levels of enrollment is bound to be a consideration in the bargain struck. Second, unlike consumers generally, students are present at the workplace, and their vocal opposition to tuition (price) increases places a considerable restraint on management's ability to raise prices. Finally, students are increasingly organizing into lobbies at the state and national levels. Indeed the existence of the legislation is testimonial to the effectiveness of active student lobbies. Thus, far more than the average consumer, students can have a significant impact at the legislative level; it is the legislature that must fund the cost items proposed by the parties and that typically also has the final say as to the price of the educational product.

This suggests that the injection of students into the faculty bargaining process is misdirected if tuition is the primary concern. Tuition levels are not decided in the bargaining process. They may be affected by it, but they are also affected by bargaining with suppliers of services and materials to the university and, of much greater importance, by the willingness of the legislature to subsidize tuition levels. Moreover, in many cases tuition costs are not actually borne by the students, but by their parents, who are at the same time the taxpayers who eventually subsidize tax-supported institutions. The true cost of collective bargaining, therefore, is a matter of equal or greater concern to the public at large, whose representative is the government that bargains for and funds the final package.

The second argument for special provision for student participation in faculty bargaining is more difficult. Both experience and logic indicate that concern for student participation in academic government provides the real motivation for such provisions. There has been no experience with student participation in collective bargaining in the states in which statutory provisions exist, but there has been extensive student participation in one state without statutory authorization—Massachusetts. Thus it is the Massachusetts experience, more than anything else, which has seemed to provide the model for the student efforts for statutory recognition of their role.

In Massachusetts, collective bargaining at the organized campuses of the state college system, which began in 1970 at Boston State College, has focused largely on academic government for essentially two reasons. First, the Massachusetts statute, until 1974, limited bargaining by state employees to "conditions of employment,"[163] and this was construed to exclude the usual statutory concomitants, wages and hours. Second, few of the organized campuses had well-established, strongly supported faculty senates or other forms of governance. Thus collective bargaining became the primary mechanism by which faculty input into academic government was achieved. The board of trustees of the system, when they agreed that governance should be a subject to be negotiated, took the position that students should be included in the governing structures to be created and should therefore be involved in bargaining. The faculty organizations did not all agree, but each campus, whether or not a student was present at the bargaining table, executed collective agreements specifying the right of students to representation on curriculum, calendar, budget development, admissions, and similar committees.[164] This result apparently provides the model in student lobbying for such provisions as those in Oregon, Montana, and Maine.

Our purpose here is not to enter the thicket of the controversy about the proper role of students in academic government. For pres-

[163]*Mass. Gen. Laws*, Ch. 149, § 178F (6) (repealed 1974).

[164]The description to 1974 is that of the major proponent of student involvement, Donald E. Walters, Deputy Provost of the Massachusetts State College System. Collective Bargaining in Higher Education, Proceedings, 2d Annual Conference, National Center for the Study of Collective Bargaining in Higher Education, Baruch College 97-101 (1974).

ent purposes, we may assume that it is entirely appropriate that students have such a role, that they not be regarded as mere consumers of an educational product, but as active participants in the educational process. It does not follow, however, that they should have a defined and separate role in faculty collective bargaining. That consequence would follow, indeed, if one were to assume that the role of faculty collective bargaining is to establish a union mechanism to displace the traditional forms of faculty participation. If curriculum, admissions, grading, promotion and tenure, and similar questions are to be decided through the union machinery established by, and a continuing part of, the collective bargaining process, then it may well be argued that students should have a voice in that process. It is our view, however, that a collective bargaining statute should not be so structured as to ensure or even encourage this result but should, on the contrary, provide a framework that will encourage the more traditional forms of faculty participation in academic government. For reasons we have indicated earlier, we think it is neither feasible nor desirable to legislatively mandate this result by restricting the scope of bargaining. But it is possible to structure the bargaining unit to maximize the possibility that academic matters will continue to be governed through the established machinery.

If we assume a statute so constructed, and if we are correct in concluding that with that kind of structure it is entirely probable that academic decisions will continue to be made in the traditional way, it is both unnecessary and potentially highly dangerous to provide for student participation in the collective bargaining process. It is unnecessary because student participation can be effected and will be effected, to the extent desirable, through the normal functioning of academic government, as has been the experience. It is highly dangerous because the introduction of students into the bargaining process will of itself tend to inject into that process considerations of the details of academic governance, such as student evaluations, grading systems, and the like, that might otherwise be left by the administration and the bargaining agent to decision in the traditional way. In other words, forcible injection of students into the collective bargaining process can be justified only on the assumption that that process will involve itself in the details of academic government; if the statute mandates the inclusion of students it may indeed ensure that the premise will be the fact, where, in their absence, it would not be. Thus it is interesting to note that after the Massachusetts statute was revised, effective July 1, 1974, to include "wages, hours, standards of productivity and performance, and any other terms and conditions of employment,"[165] students were excluded from the bargaining process in those state colleges where they had actively participated when the scope of bargaining was confined largely to governance issues.[166]

There is as yet no experience with statutorily mandated student participation in faculty collective bargaining. There is, however, considerable experience with the movement toward enlarged student participation in academic decision-making. That experience strongly suggests that special statutory provisions are unnecessary for the achievement of the legitimate goals of that movement and may, in fact, jeopardize the achievement of a bargaining structure that will permit faculty to seek to protect their employee interests while preserving the academic government under which the student role in many institutions has greatly enlarged.

Representation Elections

Under virtually all statutes providing for the selection of an exclusive bargaining agent the affirmative vote of a majority of those voting (or, under the Railway Labor Act, of those eligible to vote) is required before a particular organization can be designated as the bargaining agent. In all statutes one of the choices offered to the electorate is not to have collective bargaining at all by voting for "no agent"[167] (or, under the Railway Labor Act, by not voting). Thus, when two or more organizations are competing for designation as the bargaining representative there are at least three possible choices for every voter. The standard method for dealing with the possibility that none of the entries will command a majority is to provide for a run-off between

---

[165]*Mass. Gen. Laws* Ch. 150E, § 6, as added by St. 1973, Ch. 1078, Sec. 2, effective July 1, 1974.

[166]Telephone interview with Donald E. Walters, former Deputy Provost of the Massachusetts State College System, July 20, 1976.

[167]Under the NLRB, the no-agent choice is variously labelled, depending on the number of competing organizations. If only one organization is seeking representation rights the vote is either "for" or "against" it; if two are, the no-agent choice is labelled "neither"; if three are, it is "none." For convenience we will refer to the vote against any representation as "no agent."

the entries that ran first and second in the first balloting. The contenders in the run-off may be an employee organization and the "no agent" entry, or they may be the two leading employee organizations.[168]

The possibility of not having a "no agent" entry in the run-off has appeared to create a problem for some. When this occurs, a particular organization can theoretically win bargaining rights even though a majority of the electorate would prefer "no agent" to that organization. This can occur under the following conditions: (1) less than a third of the electorate prefer "no agent" to either of the contenders, and (2) the number of those supporting the loser in the run-off who would have preferred "no agent" to the winner is sufficiently large so that, when added to those who prefer "no agent" to either, they constitute a majority. For example, if 35 percent prefer organization A, 35 percent prefer organization B, and 30 percent prefer no organization at all, there will be a run-off between A and B in which those who voted "no agent" will be the deciding factor. If A wins, and if 60 percent of those supporting B in the first election would have preferred "no agent" to A, A will be the exclusive bargaining representative even though a majority would have preferred "no agent" to it if given an opportunity to make that choice.

In an apparent effort to meet this possibility Oregon has provided that higher education faculty elections shall have two stages simultaneously.[169] The faculty is first asked to decide whether it wants collective bargaining or not. On the same ballot it is asked to pick among the competing organizations. If a majority answers the first question in the negative, the second part of the ballot is ignored. If the answer to the first question is in the affirmative, then the choice is made from among the competing organizations. If none receives a

---

[168]This is prescribed by Section 9(c)(3) of the National Labor Relations Act, as amended in 1947, 29 U.S.C. § 189(c)(3). Prior to 1947 the Board's practice was to eliminate the "no agent" choice from the run-off unless it had the most votes in the first election. National Labor Relations Board, *Rules and Regulations, Series 4*, 29 Fed. Reg. Ch. 11, § 203.56(c) (1946). This was condemned by both those supporting and opposing the Taft-Hartley Act. See House Rept. No. 245 on H.R. 3020, 80th Cong., 1st Sess., 38 (1947); Sen. Rept. No. 105 on S. 1126, 80th Cong., 1st Sess., 12, 25 (1947); Sen. Min. Rept. No. 105, 80th Cong., 1st Sess., 41 (1947); House Conf. Rept. No. 510 on H.R. 3020, 80th Cong., 1st Sess., 48 (1947).

[169]*Ore. Rev. Stat.* § 243.686 (6) (1975).

majority, a run-off is also held between the two organizations securing the most votes in the first election. Iowa also requires the two-
stage election procedure, but for all employees covered by the state
Act.[170] The Vermont labor board has interpreted the state's Act as
requiring a similar arrangement for state employees, but in which
"no agent" also appears on the second part of the ballot.[171]

It is difficult to understand the justification for the Oregon procedure. In the case in which the traditional run-off procedure would
produce a choice not preferred by a majority if it had an opportunity
to select "no agent" as an alternative, the Oregon procedure would
produce the same result if the electors voted their genuine preferences
on the first ballot. Further, the Oregon procedure can produce an
erroneous result in a great many configurations in which the traditional system will not. What it amounts to is a first ballot in which all
of those favoring collective bargaining by any of the competing organizations are matched against those who prefer to have none of them.
Then, if those opposed to collective bargaining do not succeed in
obtaining a majority, they are forced to choose among the competing
organizations. In the traditional system, the choices, including "no
agent," having the least support are eliminated; in the Oregon system
the "no agent" vote is eliminated. Since the "no agent" vote can be as
high as 49.9 percent the chances of a theoretically erroneous result are
obviously greatly enhanced.

The Vermont system does not enlarge the possibility of error,
since it replicates the traditional system if the answer to the first question is in the affirmative, thus providing two opportunities to vote for
"no agent." It does not, however, meet the supposed problem. Indeed,
neither system will lead to a theoretically better result than the traditional system (and the Oregon system can lead to a worse) if the electors vote their real preferences.

What the two systems appear to accomplish is to give those who
really prefer collective bargaining, but who fear that their chosen representative will lose, an opportunity to vote against collective bargaining so that the contest in which their preferred organization may

[170]*Iowa Code Ann.* § 20.15 (1976 Supp.).

[171]Telephone interview with Evan C. Archer, Jr., Attorney to the Vermont State
Employees Labor Relations Board, June 29, 1976.

lose will not take place.[172] But the same opportunity can be given under the traditional system with much less danger of an erroneous result: Supporters of a particular organization who anticipate that it will not have sufficient support to get into the run-off, or that it will lose the run-off, can vote for "no agent" in the first election. The vice of the Oregon, Iowa, and Vermont systems is that by asking an abstract question they encourage voters not to mark their ballots based on their real preferences but, instead, to vote in accordance with their anticipation of how others will vote. In particular, they seem designed to induce voters who prefer collective bargaining, but who anticipate that their preferred agent will lose, to vote against collective bargaining. Any system designed to encourage voters to falsify their preferences because of their possibly inaccurate estimation of how others will vote is obviously undesirable.

There is a system that would answer the theoretical imperfection of the traditional rerun procedure. That system would use a single ballot and ask each voter to indicate a series of choices, including "no agent," in order of preference. If no majority winner appears among the first choices the entry receiving the least number of votes would be eliminated and the ballots cast for that entry redistributed to the second choices, the process continuing until one of the entries has achieved a majority. This system, although used in many kinds of elections, has never been used, as far as we know, in the choice of a collective bargaining representative. The reason is that although it does

---

[172]This is a somewhat more analytical statement than the first published justification of an Oregon-type procedure that we have found. R. Carr and D. Van Eyck, *Collective Bargaining Comes to Campus* (Washington, D.C.: American Council on Education, 1973), pp. 69–70, argue that some faculty members who oppose collective bargaining nevertheless feel constrained to vote for one organization because of the fear that two other organizations would otherwise be the contenders in any run-off. They propose the preliminary yes or no election as the solution. What they do not explain is why, in any rational constituency in which it is anticipated that less than one-third will vote for "no agent" in an election of the traditional kind, a majority will vote that way on a preliminary ballot. Indeed, the example they provide to show the "logic" of the use of the preliminary yes or no ballot argues, if anything, against it. At Youngstown State University (Ohio), in an Oregon-style election conducted without benefit of statute, less than 23 percent voted against collective bargaining, but almost 45 percent opposed the agent finally selected. One can speculate about the "logic" of such a system if 45 percent had voted against collective bargaining on the preliminary ballot and the voters were then forced to choose between the contending organizations rather than between "no agent" and the leading contender.

eliminate the possibility of designating a representative who would have been opposed by a majority if given the "no agent" alternative in the run-off, it eliminates one very useful characteristic of the traditional system, that is, the opportunity for the electorate to reconsider the alternatives after the first ballot has failed to produce a majority winner. The organizations remaining in the contest at that point can make adjustments or alliances with groups in the unit and arguments can be addressed to the electorate concerning the remaining choices. On the first ballot the competing organizations must in effect campaign against "no agent" as well as against each other. Depending on how well they guess the identity of the prime rival, the competing organizations, and indeed those supporting no organization, may direct their campaign toward the wrong target. After a first election in which no majority winner appears there is an opportunity to refocus the campaign and to supply information bearing directly on the remaining alternatives. The result is, in the end, a better-informed electorate and, perhaps, a more rational choice. It is for this reason, we believe, that the traditional system has, except in the two instances noted, been adopted in all state statutes.

In any case, no particular characteristic of higher education seems to call for a different balloting system than the one adjudged to be desirable for all other public employees or, for that matter, for employees in the private sector. The Oregon system has only one possible justification: it allows faculty who oppose collective bargaining in effect to capture on the first question those who prefer collective bargaining, and would not therefore vote "no agent," but who anticipate that their choice of agents would not win the election. Only in that event will that system produce a negative vote on the first question where the traditional system would elect a bargaining representative.

Union Security

Union security is a phrase applied to a variety of devices employed to assure the bargaining agent's financial support and stability; among the more prominent are the union shop and the agency shop. Under the former the employer agrees with the bargaining agent that all employees must, as a condition of employment, join the organization. Under the latter the employer agrees with the bargaining agent that all nonmember employees must, as a condition of employment, pay an amount equivalent to union dues and fees in lieu of actual membership. Under the National Labor Relations Act, however, in neither arrangement can the employer discharge an employee other than for his failure to pay union dues and the initiation fee;[173] thus in the private sector the union and agency shops are for all practical purposes equivalent. Moreover, the United States Supreme Court sustained the Railway Labor Act against constitutional challenge based on the employee's first amendment right not to be compelled to contribute to political causes supported by the union with dues exacted under a statutorily permissible union security provision.[174] The Court construed the Act as prohibiting the union from expending dues, over a member's objection, to support political causes that he opposes. Although the question is not exactly the same under the National Labor Relations Act since, unlike the Railway Labor Act, the NLRA does not legitimize an agency shop otherwise unlawful under state law, it is generally assumed that it would be similarly construed. In any event there is little doubt about the constitutionality of union security in the private sector.

In the public sector, however, the issue of union security has generated considerable controversy,[175] much of it centered on constitutional grounds. Some state laws omit the NLRA's proviso limiting an employer's right to discharge an employee under a union security provision to the failure to pay dues and fees; thus a serious constitutional question of freedom of association would arise in the event the state act is construed as permitting the parties to require actual membership as opposed to the tendering of dues as a condition of employment. Moreover, even where an agency shop may be expressly authorized, inasmuch as public sector bargaining is so closely intertwined with the political process the problem of the use of union dues for "political" purposes is seriously compounded. A Michigan court recently sustained that state's statutorily authorized agency shop against first amendment challenge by reading it as consistent with the

[173]29 U.S.C. § 158 (a) (3) (1970).

[174]International Ass'n of Machinists v. Street, 367 U.S. 740 (1961).

[175]See generally, P. N. Blair, "Union Security Agreements in Public Employment," 60 *Cornell L. Rev.* 183 (1975).

private sector law.[176] However, that approach poses the rather difficult problem of distinguishing impermissible support of political causes to which a unit member may properly object from legitimate political activity in furtherance of the organization's collective bargaining goals. The United States Supreme Court has decided to hear the case.

A second set of issues is purely statutory. In some states the collective bargaining law's failure to speak to union security coupled with a statutory right to refrain from engaging in or supporting union activity has resulted in the prohibition of the agency shop. Furthermore, under civil service or teacher tenure laws, permanent employees cannot be dismissed except for just cause; as a result the question arises as to whether the failure to pay dues and fees constitutes grounds for dismissal or whether a union security provision negotiated under the collective bargaining law controls in any conflict with a civil service or teacher tenure law. Finally, an issue that has only recently emerged is whether the 1972 amendment to Title VII of the Civil Rights Act of 1964, requiring employers in both the public and private sectors to make reasonable accommodations to an employee's religious observance, requires some exemption or special treatment of employees who object to payment of union fees on religious grounds.

Minnesota and Hawaii have dealt with both the political-use and grounds-for-discharge problems by statute. Both provide for mandatory "fair share" deductions for nonmembers.[177] Because the deduction is automatic and imposed by statute rather than as a result of a collective agreement the grounds-for-discharge problem is obviated, since the individual is not given the opportunity not to make payment. The "fair share" requirement ties the amount of the deduction to the cost of services rendered as exclusive bargaining agent. Administratively, however, the acts differ. In Hawaii the PERB must first approve the fair-share service fee. In Minnesota the judiciary would determine in individually contested cases whether the amount charged is permissible, and the Minnesota Supreme Court recently sustained the provision against a due process challenge, although it

[176]Abood v. Detroit Bd. of Ed., 230 N.W. 2d 322 (Mich. Ct. App. 1975), cert. granted 425 U.S. 949 (1976).

[177]*Minn. Stat.* § 176.65(2) (1976 Supp.); *Hawaii Rev. Stat.* § 89-4 (1975 Supp.).

commended the Hawaii approach to the legislature.[178] Massachusetts allows the parties to agree to a fair-share deduction subject to the vote of the bargaining unit, not just the members of the organization.[179] Oregon and Montana allow for the union or agency shop, but require that employees who object on religious grounds be allowed instead to make a contribution in lieu of dues to a charitable organization.[180]

Two arguments can be made against allowing union or agency shops in higher education. First, the dismissal of a teacher for failure to tender union dues and fees would not be based on "adequate cause" as that term is understood in higher education; that is, it would have nothing to do with the professor's professional competence. Second, a termination for failure to authorize the deduction of the fee on grounds of conscientious objection to unionization would constitute a violation of academic freedom. We believe neither assertion to be sound. Academic freedom substantively protects the individual's right not to be dismissed for his or her teaching or writing, subject only to an adherence to professional standards. An agency shop would not interfere substantively with a professor's exercise of academic freedom. To the extent that academic freedom has also been understood to protect the faculty member from institutional action based on the exercise of his civil liberties, we see no infringement in the operation of a permissible union security device; the faculty member, while compelled to support the bargaining agent, may, if he chooses, remain a vocal opponent of the organization or of collective bargaining in general. Further, faculty appointments may terminate on grounds other than personal competence if some appropriate countervailing policy not infringing academic freedom or constitutional rights permits. For example, an appointment may terminate on grounds of age whether or not the incumbent is still perfectly competent. Accordingly, the question is whether there are compelling countervailing considerations.

Several considerations supporting union security are applicable to all employees, including faculties in higher education. First,

[178]Robbinsdale Educ. Ass'n v. Robbinsdale Fed. of Teachers, 239 N.W. 2d 439 (Minn. 1976).

[179]*Mass. Gen. Laws* Ch. 150E, § 12 (1976).

[180]*Ore. Rev. Stat.* § 243.666(1) (1975), *Mont. Rev. Code* § 59-1603(5) (1975 Cum. Supp.).

employees who derive the benefits of collective bargaining should bear their share of the cost. Second, a financially secure union may be a more responsible union. It will not need to constantly demonstrate its militance to secure employee support. As a result it is actually to the employer's benefit to allow for union security. Third, a financially unstable union may encourage a more obstinate bargaining stance by the employer, which in turn may contribute to a deterioration in labor relations.

There is, however, an additional reason, particular to higher education, for allowing union security. In our discussion of the bargaining unit we have argued that the constituency for the selection of a bargaining agent should be substantially identical to the polity for academic government if governance and bargaining are to be harmonized. This is, we believe, a necessary but not a sufficient condition. It is of equal importance that a bargaining representative be responsive to the entire constituency it represents, not just that portion, even if a majority, that chose it. If the constituencies of the academic senate and collective bargaining structures differ substantially, the likelihood of conflict and, more important, of a struggle for dominance by one or the other is greatly enlarged. If membership in the academic constituency is compulsory, as it is, and support of the collective bargaining agency is voluntary, there almost necessarily will result a continuing effort by the collective bargaining agent to demonstrate its power and its effectiveness to obtain and retain its financial support, and that effort may well impel it to seek to displace the academic structure rather than to negotiate for its continued existence. A union or agency shop, on the other hand, will encourage greater participation in the bargaining organization by unit members and thereby produce a bargaining program more reflective of the academic interests of the unit as a whole. It also benefits the institutional employer to treat with a more fully representative bargaining agent.

While the arguments supporting the union or agency shop on campus far outweigh the arguments mustered in opposition, discharging a faculty member because his beliefs prevent him from authorizing an agency fee seems altogether too severe. Thus, we believe it advisable to accommodate the true conscientious objector. Accordingly, we shall make such a proposal in Chapter Three.

3

Proposed Statutory Provisions

As noted in the Overview, many issues have to be resolved in drafting a public employee bargaining law. Some of them, such as whether there will be a three- or a five-person board, whether there shall be a separate general counsel's office, or how collective bargaining agreements may be enforced, are not highly charged; others, such as impasse procedures and the right to strike, are. The resolution of those issues, while important, is not of special significance for higher education. What follows, therefore, is not a model law but the specific provisions that we recommend be included in a public employee bargaining law because of the distinctive character of faculty employer-employee relationships in higher education, irrespective of how the issues not having such special relevance are resolved. There is no provision for a special balloting procedure or for a student role in the bargaining process because, for the reasons stated in Chapter Two, we believe such provisions are unwarranted if not pernicious.

The recommended provisions assume that the statute in which they are to be included is a general statute governing collective bargaining for public employees or one covering all of education, rather than a specific statute dealing only with faculty in higher education. Many of the recommended provisions are therefore in the form of provisos to provisions having broader application. In some recommendations, general descriptive language is used, because each state has its own particular terminology, which could, and should, be substituted. The recommended provisions are in many instances, therefore, intended as guides rather than as finished products that can be inserted in a statute in *haec verba*.

Definition of a "Labor Organization" or "Employee Organization"
Most state laws follow the NLRA's prohibition on "company unionism," which makes it an unfair labor practice for an employer to dominate, interfere in, or support a labor organization. The goal is to assure that employees will be represented by an organization of their own choosing. Moreover, the federal definition of a labor organization is quite broad including any organization *of any kind* that exists for the purpose in whole or in part of *dealing* with the employer. The National Labor Relations Board has held that a faculty senate is not a labor organization under the Act.[181] A latent danger is that a university administration will be prohibited from participating in or supporting duly established faculty governing bodies by a more mechanical reading of similar language in a state law. Accordingly, prudence suggests that the definition of an employee organization preclude such a reading. On the other hand, in making unit determinations the exclusion of senates (or similar bodies however named in the particular institution) should not prevent reference to the past activities of such bodies as representatives of faculty. The history of employee representation is often explicitly referred to in state statutes as one of the criteria to be used in unit determination, and it is a primary determinant under the National Labor Relations Act, although it is not mentioned. It is therefore of critical importance that the senate structure be considered in making unit determinations for faculty bargaining.

RECOMMENDED PROVISION 1
An "employee organization" is any organization of any kind in which employees participate and which exists for the purpose in whole or in part of collective bargaining with the public employer; *provided* that, except for the purpose of determining the history of employee representation in a unit determination, any committee, council, senate, or other such body in any institution of higher educa-

[181]Northwestern University, 218 NLRB No. 40 (1975).

tion in which faculty participate in whole or in part and which serves as part of the internal governing structure of such institution shall not be deemed an employee organization.

Comment. In a particular state statute it may be desirable to substitute the appropriate section reference for the words "in a unit determination."

Definition of a "Supervisor"

Whether or not the state chooses to exclude supervisors from rank-and-file units or exempt them from collective bargaining is of no particular moment to higher education so long as the integrity of the core faculty and its leaders is retained for bargaining unit purposes. The earlier discussion underlined the importance of retaining the "academic focus" of the bargaining unit, which should include those faculty who might be understood to perform supervisory functions. The NLRB has managed to accommodate many of these academic concerns under a rather rigid statute but, again, it would be well for a state bargaining law to reflect the policy more directly.

RECOMMENDED PROVISION 2

A "supervisor" is any individual having authority, in the interest of the employer, to hire, transfer, suspend, lay off, recall, promote, discharge, assign, reward, or discipline other employees, or responsibly to direct them, or to adjust their grievances, or effectively to recommend such action if in connection with the foregoing the exercise of such authority is not of a merely routine or clerical nature, but requires the use of independent judgment; *provided* that in an institution of higher education, any chairman, director, coordinator, principal investigator, or other leader of an academic unit, component, or program who performs any of the above duties primarily in the interest of members of the academic unit, component, or program or who supervises any persons not included in the bargaining unit shall not be deemed a supervisor for that reason.

Definition of "Managerial Employee"

Although not mentioned in the Act itself, managerial employees have, like supervisors, been excluded from representation rights under the National Labor Relations Act by judicial decision.[182] Regardless of whether a state statute attempts to codify such exclusion or to allow managerial personnel to form separate bargaining units, there is a danger that members of the faculty, or members of faculty committees, who exercise discretion in the conduct of the educational enterprise may fall within the definition of managerial employees. Again, the importance of maintaining the integrity of the core faculty for unit purposes suggests that some legislative provision may be needed.

RECOMMENDED PROVISION 3

"Managerial employee" means any employee having significant discretionary responsibilities for formulating or administering policies and programs on behalf of the public employer; *provided* that in an institution of higher education no employee or group of employees shall be deemed to be managerial employees because the employee or group of employees participates in decisions with respect to courses, curriculum, personnel, or other matters of educational policy.

Determination of an Appropriate Bargaining Unit

The statute should distinguish between the determination of an appropriate bargaining unit, really the election district for which the would-be bargaining agents must compete, and the actual bargaining structure that may eventually develop. Thus it should reject the notion that some perfect or most appropriate unit exists. That approach would require the board to visualize the bargaining process in advance, to weigh the pros and cons of various bargaining structures and to decide which is the most preferable. The result, usually coupled with a policy that favors more comprehensive bargaining units, makes organizing more difficult and, more important, simply lumps diverse groups together. Thus it shifts the burden on the bargaining agent to accommodate more competing interests than its internal political processes can reasonably withstand. The educational impact of such homogenization may be devastating. Accordingly, a better policy, attuned to achieving a workable adjustment of bargaining and faculty government, is to make the faculty governance constituency the polity for the bargaining election and to make it clear that the unit so defined is not the only unit in which bargain-

[182]NLRB v. Bell Aerospace Co., 416 U.S. 267 (1974).

ing can take place. As the following section will show, the public employer's interest in a rational bargaining structure can be accommodated while the election district decision conforms to a true community of academic interest. Thus, in any given jurisdiction the statute could itself identify that community (for example, the core faculty of each campus of the state college or university system) and legislate each of them as an election district. Indeed geographic scope is an issue solely for multicampus systems. In any event the number of public institutions of higher education in any state is not so great that specific legislative determination of the issue would be impracticable. Thus, in Wisconsin, the Regents Task Force on University Governance and Collective Bargaining recommended that the statute provide that each campus of the University of Wisconsin system be deemed an appropriate unit. Such a solution may, however, not be politically practicable in a general statute because it would lead to demands by other groups for legislative determination of bargaining units. General language that would guide a public employment relations board may therefore be desirable.

The following recommendation contains two significant elements for higher education. It lists the criteria commonly used in state unit determination provisions but includes, as one element, the structure of academic government. This provides some flexibility. For those systems that exhibit a high degree of centralized control and whose campuses are, essentially, branches of a unitarily governed institution, this recommendation would permit the labor board to find a single unit appropriate. On the other hand, in such institutions as the University of California, where each campus exercises substantial autonomy in academic decision making, it would permit separate campus units.

The second major element is the prohibition of inclusion by the PERB of faculty and nonfaculty in a single unit, whatever the geographic determination, except where a majority of both groups desire such a broader unit. This is modelled after, and included with, the provision dealing with professional employees copied from the National Labor Relations Act. Unlike that provision, which requires the consent only of the professionals for an all-inclusive unit, the recommended language requires the consent of both groups.

Finally, by specifying that a unit can be found to be appropriate even if another unit might also be appropriate, the recommended provision makes it clear that the statute does not mandate a particular bargaining structure, but allows the parties, within the limits of the permissibly appropriate units, to create their own structure. The following provides more general language toward the same end. It should be noted that the "history of representation" criterion dovetails with the definition of an employee organization proposed in Recommended Provision 2.

RECOMMENDED PROVISION 4

In determining an appropriate unit, the Public Employment Relations Board shall consider the community of interest of employees, including occupational community of interest, the commonality of terms and conditions of employment, common supervision, degree of interchange, geographic separation, extent of organization, and history of representation in the division or subdivision of the employer involved, and, in any institution of higher education, the structure of academic government; *provided* that in any state college or university no unit shall include both faculty and nonfaculty [as defined by the institution's governance structure][183] unless a majority of each group, voting separately, approve representation in such a broader unit; *and provided* that no unit shall include both professional and nonprofessional employees unless a majority of such professional employees vote for inclusion in such unit. The board may determine a unit to be appropriate in a particular case even though some other unit might also be appropriate.

Bargaining Structure

As a concomitant of the above, the statute should make plain that combinations of various bargaining units can cluster for bargaining purposes or, alternatively, that the public employer can require joint bargaining on issues of statewide impact or engage in "pattern" bargaining if the labor organizations refuse to form a coalition. In this way management can rationalize its bargaining structure, avoiding whipsawing or leapfrogging, while each representative retains a duty solely to its local constituency. Moreover, accommodations made

[183]It should be noted that further definition may be required. The intention is to restrict "faculty" to those who participate in governance.

between bargaining representatives can be made armslength and not by submerging interests within all-inclusive units.

There are various mechanical ways of achieving this objective. The most convenient is to use the definition of *the duty to bargain*. This can be placed either in the definition section of the statute or, as in the National Labor Relations Act, be made part of the unfair labor practice provisions. The following provision follows the latter model and assumes that there is in the statute a provision, comparable to Section 8(a)(5) of the National Labor Relations Act, making it an unfair labor practice for the public employer to refuse to bargain in good faith with a certified or recognized collective bargaining representative and a comparable provision imposing a duty to bargain in good faith upon a certified or recognized representative. The recommended provision, as framed, deals with any public employer. It can be modified, if desired, to apply only to institutions of higher education.

RECOMMENDED PROVISION 5

It shall not be an unfair labor practice:

(a) for a public employer and a labor organization representing employees in two or more bargaining units to agree to merge such units into a single unit for the purpose of collective bargaining, if the employees involved could appropriately have been included within a single bargaining unit;

(b) for a public employer (i) to demand joint bargaining by two or more employee organizations with respect to matters which have customarily been provided on a uniform basis among the employees represented by such labor organizations, or (ii) if joint bargaining is not agreed to by those employee organizations or no agreement is reached acceptable to all parties, to conclude an agreement as to such matters with the organization or organizations which represent the largest number of employees and to refuse to bargain further with any other organizations as to such matters unless that other organization agrees to accept the terms so negotiated.

(c) for two or more employee organizations to demand joint bargaining with a public employer with respect to matters which have customarily been provided on a uniform basis among the employees represented by such employee organizations.

Comment. Paragraph (a) of the above provision gives express statutory sanction to what is the law, without such express sanction, under the National Labor Relations Act. Under the Act the NLRB considers bargaining history when making a unit determination. If a union, although separately certified for a number of plant units in a multiplant company, has in fact carried on bargaining with the employer on a unitary basis, and the agreement made with the employer is a single contract that "contains all the substantive ground rules," even if supplemented by local agreements on plant issues, the Board will find that the parties have created a single companywide unit at all plants at which the union is the bargaining representative.[184] This will bar single-plant elections.[185] Where some of the major substantive issues are separately bargained, the parties must indicate clearly their intention to create a single unit.[186] This doctrine has been criticized on the ground that it is, essentially, a one-way process permitting a merger of units that the Board has found separately appropriate in ordering elections but not permitting employees in the constituent units to withdraw when they become dissatisfied with the merged bargaining.[187] Whatever the merits of the criticism in the private sector, the acknowledged desirability of minimizing the multiplicity of units in public employment seems to us to warrant adoption of the NLRB rule and its explicit incorporation into the statute so long as the resulting combined unit is an appropriate one.

Paragraphs (b) and (c) represent a departure from what at least appears to be the law under the National Labor Relations Act. Under the Act the parties may jointly agree to merge separate units, but the NLRB holds that a demand by either party for joint bargaining or a merger of units is not a mandatory subject of bargaining, with the result that insistence to impasse upon joint bargaining, or even making the agreement for one unit conditional on satisfactory conclusion of negotiations as to another unit, constitutes an unfair labor prac-

[184]General Motors Corp. 120 NLRB 1215, 1220 (1958); Chase Brass & Copper Co., 123 NLRB 1032 (1959).

[185]Owens-Illinois Glass Co., 108 NLRB 947 (1954).

[186]American Can Co., 109 NLRB 128 (1954), 114 NLRB 1547 (1955).

[187]G. W. Brooks and M. Thompson, "Multi-plant Units: The NLRB's Withdrawal of Free Choice," 20 *Industrial and Labor Relations Review*, 363 (1967).

tice.[188] The justification for the departure from Board precedent is the acknowledged desirability of avoiding in public employment the whipsawing that can result from a multiplicity of bargaining units. As we have indicated, many statutes have sought to meet this problem by mandating large bargaining units. Our view is that the creation of large units that contain diverse elements would be most harmful in institutions of higher education. The above proposals, building on the approach of the Oregon Act, appear to us to provide a method for dealing with the whipsawing problem without sacrificing the interests of institutional governance in higher education.

Note that while paragraph (a) authorizes total merger of bargaining units by consent, paragraphs (b) and (c)—which in effect make joint bargaining a mandatory subject of bargaining—and paragraph (b) which gives the employer the power to impose it, even if not agreed to—are limited to issues that have customarily been settled on a uniform basis. In a multicampus university, for example, which traditionally has a single salary schedule for all campuses, but which deals with other matters on a campus-by-campus basis, the university administration could insist upon a uniform agreement on changes in salary schedules, and if not agreed to, could make an agreement with the largest unit and refuse to bargain further with the others only on that subject; on matters that have traditionally been dealt with on a campus basis, with differing results, the administration would have no right to impose uniformity. The provision also makes clear that the employer cannot, after joint bargaining, take advantage of the permissible pattern bargain by settling with the weaker organizations (at least in terms of the total number of employees represented) and imposing that settlement on the stronger. For the same reason the employer cannot impose terms on an organization to which the demand for joint bargaining had not been directed or which had not been a participant in unsuccessful joint bargaining. The provision

[188]See F. W. Woolworth Co., 179 NLRB 748 (1969), United Steelworkers of America (Kennecott Copper Corp.) Case No. 27-CB-453, 1969 Daily Labor Reports No. 27 B-1 (Feb. 10, 1969). AFL-CIO Joint Negotiating Committee v. NLRB 184 NLRB 976 (1970), *enforcement denied* 459 F. 2d 374 (3rd Cir. 1972).

See also Shell Oil Co., 194 NLRB 988 *pet. rew. denied*, OCAW v. NLRB 486 F. 2d 1266 (D.C. Cir. 1973), and Standard Oil Co., 137 NLRB 690, *enforced* 322 F. 2d 40 (6th Cir. 1963).

does, however, give real meaning to the joint bargaining procedure, because a settlement with a coalition representing the largest number could be binding even on the nonconsenting representative of the single largest unit. As a result, the bargaining agents are under considerable pressure to come together and arrive at a mutually acceptable resolution.

Scope of Bargaining

At the outset we reject the "forbidden-permitted" approach as unsupportable on both doctrinal and practical grounds. Doctrinally, it holds that the public employer cannot agree to terms of a collective agreement that limits its power to exercise governmental authority; thus it fails to perceive that the governmental employer retains the ability to control the terms of the bargain subject only to whatever impasse provisions the state wishes to make. Moreover, the doctrine should logically prohibit any public employer from engaging any public employee on any terms other than a moment-to-moment hiring at will, since contracting for services for any longer duration or on any other specific term perforce curtails the employer's ability to take unilateral action. While some older support may be found even for disallowing a public employer to appoint for a period of a year, as a derogation of its sovereign power, few modern jurisdictions would embrace it.

Practically, this approach ultimately rests on the assumption that public employee unions will have "too much" power unless their scope of bargaining is narrowed. We do not believe that recent experience necessarily bears out this judgment; nor do we believe that unions bargain tenaciously on controversial issues of social policy about which their members will invariably have many views. To be sure, because public employee bargaining perforce bears on the level, quality, and efficiency of social services, the issues raised at the bargaining table will have implications for the body politic. We believe that the public employer will ultimately have to make these decisions, and that, properly structured, collective bargaining will simply represent a part of the larger political process.

While this applies to public employees generally, it has additional force in faculty bargaining. The exemption of policy matters, including the faculty role in their formulation, from the range of permissible bargaining places faculty government on a decidedly weak foundation. Logically, if such matters are "management prerogatives," then those faculty who formulate policy should be excluded from the unit as managerial personnel, but that would produce ludicrous divisions within the faculty. Further, the exemption of such matters from the scope of bargaining ignores the fact that such decisions affect faculty in the most direct fashion and that greater security for a faculty voice in institutional affairs may be one of the factors militating toward collective bargaining. Finally, such restrictions produce simply unworkable distinctions between the bargainable and the forbidden.

However, as the discussion in Chapter Two made clear, we do not believe the "mandatory-permissive" distinction is an entirely satisfactory alternative. It does limit the matters upon which the employer is forbidden to take unilateral action without first bargaining but it injects into the bargaining process itself a set of legalistic distinctions that serve no useful purpose so long as the public employer is free to reject proposals that it believes it should as a matter of policy. In the public sector the distinction can, and indeed has, led to extensive litigation that has no observable purpose and occupies time and attention better reserved to resolving the underlying dispute. In higher education in particular, the "mandatory-permissive" distinction, even if based on a definition of the words "wages, hours, and terms and conditions of employment" seems—without the limitations contained in many statutes—to make distinctions totally inappropriate in the context of actual bargaining. If based on more limited language the inappropriateness of the distinction is even clearer.

Because of these considerations, the following proposal deals separately with the conduct of bargaining and unilateral action.

RECOMMENDED PROVISION 6: SCOPE OF BARGAINING

For purposes of this Act, to bargain collectively is the performance of the mutual obligation of the public employer and the collective representative to meet, upon request, at reasonable times and confer in good faith with respect to any matter affecting or arising out of the employment relationship, or the negotiation of an agreement or any question arising thereunder, and the execution of a written contract incorporating any agreement reached if requested by either party, but such obligation does not compel either party to agree to a proposal or require the making of a concession.

RECOMMENDED PROVISION 7: MANAGEMENT RIGHTS

1. Any right a public employer might otherwise have to take action of any kind shall not be affected or limited by the obligation to bargain collectively imposed by Section _____ except as provided herein.
2. Before changing any existing policy or practice directly affecting the wages, hours, or terms and conditions of employment (including those governing employee participation in the exercise of the employer's rights) of employees represented by an exclusive bargaining representative, a public employer shall first propose such change to the bargaining representative. If agreement is not reached, the public employer may institute such proposed change after bargaining to impasse or, if the provisions for the resolution of bargaining impasses provided in this Act are invoked by the bargaining representative, after final disposition under such provisions.
3. A public employer may, by agreement with a collective bargaining representative, limit or modify any of the rights otherwise preserved by this Section. An exclusive bargaining representative may, in conjunction with such agreement, limit or modify its right to bargain with respect to the subject matter of such agreement.

Comment. In devising a provision governing the duty to bargain, the collective bargaining law confronts three related but different questions: (1) what may the parties compel one another to discuss and either agree on or bring to impasse; (2) on what matters may the employer act without being first compelled to exhaust the bargaining requirement; and (3) what are the respective rights and obligations of the parties when either believes it desirable to make a change during the agreement's term about a matter not covered in a collective agreement? The statutory proposal bears on each of these.

The recommended provision first decouples the obligation to "meet and confer" and seek to reach agreement from the obligation not to make unilateral changes in terms and conditions of employment. This is accomplished by the insertion of the words "on request" in the language dealing with the scope of bargaining and by the provision in the management rights sentence that the obligation to bargain shall not be deemed to limit any right a public employer might otherwise have to take action of any kind, subject to specified limitations.

Once management's right to take unilateral action without violating the duty to bargain is separately dealt with, the definition of the duty to bargain can be much broader than the traditional one without a concomitant restriction on an employer's freedom to act without bargaining. The recommended provision defining the scope of bargaining therefore places an obligation on each party to negotiate about anything affecting or arising out of the employment relationship if request is made.

To be sure, this approach may extend the agenda that may be ultimately subject to the impasse machinery established in the Act. Thus negotiations may be made more difficult if inexperienced parties clutter the process with trivialities proposed only for later trade-off or to satisfy interest groups within the bargaining unit. We believe that as the parties gain experience this problem will not be significant, particularly if the impasse machinery is designed to encourage responsible bargaining. A stronger criticism is that the authority to decide basic issues of social policy may be removed from the public agency responsible if demands on them are brought to impasse. If the state allows public employees to strike, we do not believe unions would do so over issues peripheral to their concern on which there is little employee unanimity, that is, which are not truly amenable to the bargaining process. If some form of fact finding or even arbitration is adopted, we doubt that fact finders and arbitrators would recommend or impose terms not already widely accepted for the kind of employees involved. In sum, we see no need to erect barriers governing the parties' ability to raise and resolve employment-generated issues at the bargaining table by artificial distinctions about what they may insist on.

While we believe that this approach is sound for all public employment, it is particularly necessary with respect to faculty bargaining in higher education. As indicated more fully in Chapter Two, the faculty are and should be concerned with much more than the bread and butter issues encompassed within the statutory phrase "wages, hours and conditions of employment." Making the obligation to meet and confer (but not to agree) depend on such nice distinctions as, for example, between class size (a management prerogative) and workload (a bargainable subject) can lead to nothing but extensive litigation and, in the end, dissatisfaction. Questions of educational policy are necessarily intertwined with questions of wages, hours, and conditions of employment. The better policy, we believe, is to place no restrictions on the bargaining process and to allow the parties themselves, either by agreeing or by disagreeing, to determine the relationship between the matters to be settled in the collective bargaining agreement and the matters to be settled through the established procedures of academic government. Both are matters of faculty concern, and the line between them should be drawn in the manner that the parties find to be most satisfactory rather than by litigation through an administrative agency or the courts.

It should be emphasized that the proposed enlargement of the scope of bargaining does not imply an obligation to reach agreement on all the matters within the scope of bargaining or place any limitation upon the employer's ability to act. As we have discussed at length in Chapter Two, the major impact of the decisions under the National Labor Relations Act, and under many state employment acts, that define mandatory and permissive subjects of bargaining has been to limit the area in which an employer must first bargain and seek agreement before taking unilateral action. Once that problem is dealt with separately, as we propose, there seems to be no reason in theory or in practice to limit the scope of what the parties are required to talk about to each other.

The problem of unilateral action is dealt with in the provision headed "Management Rights." Unlike most such provisions, which enumerate, either broadly or in detail, specific rights of management, the recommended provision in its first subsection states all-encompassingly that the obligation to bargain does not affect or limit any right a public employer might otherwise have to take action of any kind except as specified. This means that unilateral action, before bargaining, is permissible except in the limited area dealt with in the succeeding provisions. Subsection 2 of the recommended provision defines the situations in which bargaining is required before taking unilateral action, and specifies the procedure. The requirement for bargaining is limited in two ways. First, it applies only to established policies or practices. Individual changes, if made in accordance with established procedures or policies can continue to be made without bargaining. This provision is then somewhat more flexible than the parallel provision in the Oregon statute, which prohibits any unconsented-to change in existing wages, hours, or conditions of employment during the pendency of an arbitration to resolve a bargaining impasse. Second, the provision is limited to policies and practices "directly affecting" wages, hours, or conditions of employment, an area far narrower than that covered by the broad statement of the duty to bargain provided in the proposed definition of the scope of bargaining and a narrower area than that covered by the National Labor Relations Act. This narrower scope is justified where the question is not whether the employer is required to bargain with the union on request but whether an unfair labor practice is committed because the employer did not first bargain with a union even without request, before taking action. The parenthetical language, specifically including practices of employee participation, makes clear that this narrower definition is not intended to permit unilateral revision of existing systems of agency consultation without prior bargaining. While this specific addition is necessary to insulate faculty governance in higher education from unilateral action, we have phrased it more broadly so that other consultative systems concerning, for example, medical residents and interns, lawyers, museum curatorial staff, and the like, would be similarly protected.

The definition, as proposed, is not without its difficulties. There still may remain questions of interpretation of the phrase "directly affecting wages, hours, or terms and conditions of employment." But we know of no method that would ascribe a specific content to the areas intended to be covered by the statutory provision without, at the same time, eliminating the necessary flexibility. In that sense the definition is analogous to the determination of a mandatory bargaining subject under the federal NLRA. Thus, for example, the subject of pensions was generally not a subject of collective bargaining in the United States prior to the late 1940s, and it was uncertain, until the *Inland Steel* decision in 1948, that the subject matter was within the scope of "wages, hours and conditions of employment."[189] Today, the

---

[189]Inland Steel Co. v. NLRB, 170 F. 2d 247 (7th Cir. 1948).

development of collective bargaining has made it clear that pensions are within the scope of the statutory terminology, which the Supreme Court has said "has been considered to absorb and give statutory approval to the philosophy of collective bargaining as worked out in the labor movement in the United States."[190] However, under the proposed provision the issue that would be presented in litigation in unilateral action cases is not the elusive question of whether the action taken was over a mandatory as opposed to a permissive subject, but over the somewhat sharper question of whether there was an applicable past practice. (It should perhaps be noted that "past practice" is something of a term of art in labor parlance and there is a good deal of experience under contractual past-practice provisions.) The proposed language is our best effort to allow flexibility while restricting the employer's ability to effect unilateral change solely to those matters that employees traditionally rely on as ongoing terms of their service.

The first sentence of section 3 of the recommended management rights provision ensures that nothing in the prior sections, or any implicit notion of unbargainable matters, shall limit the ability of a public agency to bargain collectively. Thus, it is the management rights counterpart of the recommended provision defining an expanded scope of bargaining. It is arguably unnecessary in light of that provision, but it is recommended to avoid the possibility of the kind of judicial limitation on the permissible subjects of bargaining described in this chapter and as a necessary predicate for the second sentence, which permits limited waivers of the duty to bargain.

The third question addressed by these recommended provisions is the duty to bargain during the term of an existing collective agreement. This is, in the private industrial sector, a subject of much controversy. Under the National Labor Relations Act, as under almost all collective bargaining statutes, the duty to bargain is continuous and does not terminate with the execution of an agreement. The agreement, as one court has put it, "provides a framework within which the process of collective bargaining may be carried on."[191] This is statutorily recognized in the statement that collective bargaining

[190]Order of R.R. Telegraphers v. Railway Express Agency, 321 U.S. 342, 346 (1944).

[191]NLRB v. Highland Park Mfg. Co., 110 F. 2d 632, 638 (4th Cir. 1940).

includes the negotiation of questions arising under an agreement.

Prior to 1947, the duty to bargain was also construed as including a duty to bargain on proposed changes in matters covered by an existing, unexpired agreement.[192] The 1947 Taft-Hartley amendments specifically reversed this doctrine by specifying in Section 8(d) that the duty to bargain should not be construed as including a duty to discuss modifications of the terms of an agreement that would become effective before that agreement could be reopened under its terms. This limitation, however, as construed by the National Labor Relations Board, with the approval of the courts, does not eliminate a duty to bargain with respect to matters within the phrase "wages, hours, and conditions of employment" that are not covered by an agreement. Thus, a union demand for pensions, even during the term of an agreement, is bargainable if the agreement contains nothing about pensions.[193] This result has been much criticized.[194] It has also led to efforts to limit future bargaining by the inclusion of "zipper" clauses in many collective agreements, which in turn has led to further litigation and controversy as to the effectiveness of such provisions.[195]

As in the definition of the scope of bargaining, the question of whether there should be a duty to bargain during the term of an agreement cannot properly be resolved without looking at the different contexts in which the question arises. One of the effects of the Board's interpretation of the Section 8(d) limitation is to make unilateral action on a matter within the scope of "wages, hours, and terms and conditions of employment" but not covered by an agreement an unfair labor practice. Thus, a unilateral change in pension arrangements not covered by an agreement constitutes a violation of the duty to bargain even if there has been no request for bargaining by the union prior to the change. The critics of the Board doctrine find this result acceptable, and indeed desirable, at least as to "major terms and

[192]Carroll's Transfer Co., 56 NLRB 935 (1943).

[193]NLRB v. Jacobs Mfg. Co., 196 F. 2d 680 (2d Cir. 1952).

[194]See A. Cox and J. T. Dunlop, "The Duty to Bargain Collectively During the Term of an Existing Agreement," 63 *Harv. L. Rev.* 1097 (1950).

[195]See Westinghouse Electric Corp.; 150 NLRB 1574, 1585 (1965), and NLRB v. Southern Materials Co., 447 F. 2d 15 (4th Cir. 1971).

conditions of employment," but they would achieve that result by regarding a collective agreement as implicitly specifying that such terms and conditions should not be changed during the term of an agreement, even if not mentioned in it. Their objection to the Board doctrine is that, rather than freezing the unspecified conditions for the term of an agreement, it opens them on the one hand to union requests for bargaining and, on the other, to employer changes once the prior bargaining obligation has been met.

Since our recommended provisions separate the bargaining question *simpliciter* from the unilateral action question one could sensibly argue that the definition of the scope of bargaining should contain a provision comparable to, and perhaps broader than, the provision of Section 8(d) and that the management rights provision should forbid changes in the limited area to which the unilateral action provisions apply rather than, as we propose, simply require bargaining to impasse before any change is made. Such provisions would embody in the statute the assumption that a collective agreement for a fixed term in fact constitutes a "package" covering all existing policies or practices directly affecting wages, hours, or conditions of employment, whether or not specifically referred to in the agreement. This is, indeed, the usual assumption in private industrial employment under the National Labor Relations Act. And it is the result required by the Florida public employee bargaining law.

We believe, however, that the statute governing bargaining in the public sector should not require the parties to follow the model of comprehensive agreements for a fixed term but should permit the contrary concept, which governs bargaining under the Railway Labor Act: that is, a form of bargaining in which particular issues are dealt with as the parties feel the need to deal with them, leaving the question of whether a particular issue should be deemed settled for a fixed period to the negotiation of what is called, in bargaining under that Act, a "moratorium" agreement. The basic statutory rule under that Act is that the status quo with respect to "rates of pay, rules, or working conditions" must be maintained but that either party may, by appropriate notice, open up any particular matter for bargaining at any time. Stability is achieved by agreement, made when a particular subject has been opened, that that particular subject shall be closed to further bargaining for an agreed-upon period. Thus wage negotiations typically lead to agreements for a specified period, and a "moratorium" agreement is made that wages shall not be open to bargaining for that period. Other subjects, however, may be opened at any time, subject again to the use of the "moratorium" device to preclude further bargaining on that particular issue for whatever period the parties find appropriate. There is thus no single collective bargaining agreement for a fixed term, as is usually (but not always) the case under the National Labor Relations Act. Unilateral action is permitted, on any subject within the scope of "rates of pay, rules, or working conditions" only after the bargaining process detailed in the Act is concluded.

This is, in many respects, an attractive model. It permits great flexibility and does not impose upon the parties the necessity of settling all their problems at one time. In nonrailroad, private employment the felt need to limit the occasions when the strike weapon can be used—a need not so apparent on the railroads because of the complex, protracted, and cumbersome nature of the mandated bargaining procedures—has led to the rejection of the earlier railroad model and the prevalence of the comprehensive agreement with a fixed term. In public employment this consideration is less important. The strike weapon may be forbidden or, if permitted, may be circumscribed with such procedural devices as fact finding, compulsory mediation, and so on, in a sense comparable to those under the Railway Labor Act. Furthermore the annual public budgetary process may impose at least an annual limitation on negotiations involving monetary matters. We believe, therefore, that the statute should not impose the model of a comprehensive collective agreement, but should leave the parties free to agree on as many or as few issues as they desire and to reopen other questions when the need to do so appears.

The recommended bargaining provision thus contains no limitation comparable to Section 8(d) on bargaining during the term of an agreement. It allows the employer and union to bargain, even to impasse, on any matter arising out of the employment relationship at any time. The recommended management's rights provision does require the maintenance of the status quo in those matters that employees rely on as ongoing terms of service, but only until the union has agreed to a departure or the impasse machinery has been exhausted. They may, and most likely will, agree to a "moratorium" on many of the matters settled. Subsection 3 therefore provides that the employer's right to take action may be limited by agreement and that the collective bargaining representative may, in conjunction therewith, agree to waive its right to bargain. On other matters, for example, faculty disciplinary procedures, the parties may agree merely to a modification of existing policy but leave the subject open to further negotiations. On still others the parties may see no present need for change and simply rely on the statutory status quo. Accordingly, subsection 3 speaks of "agreement with a bargaining representative" rather than a "provision of a collective bargaining agreement."

To be sure the parties will doubtless settle kindred issues simultaneously and embody the agreement on them in a single instrument. It can, but need not, be a comprehensive collective bargaining agreement as commonly employed in industry. It could not, in the structure proposed, however, either waive the right of the employer to take action, after bargaining, on matters not covered by agreement or waive the right of the union to bargain on such matters.

These provisions have added relevance in light of the proposals on bargaining structure made earlier. Centralized coalition or pattern bargaining on economic issues may well occur against the employer's perceived need to make a single timely submission to the legislature. Before or after those issues are resolved other representatives of the "public employer" may be dealing with bargaining agents on wholly unrelated items. There should be no need to compel trade-offs between them at the highest centralized level of bargaining in order to reach a single "wrap-up" agreement.

Union Security

As we concluded in Chapter One, the policies supporting union security are fully applicable to faculty in higher education. In addition, an acceptable union security provision would be particularly useful in higher education to the extent it conduces toward greater faculty participation in the bargaining organization. However, we have also suggested that, as a matter of sound policy, faculty bargaining agents should accommodate dissenting faculty who oppose unionization on grounds of conscience; dismissal of faculty for refusal to support the bargaining agent seems far too harsh a sanction for an enterprise that prizes tolerance of personal opinion or eccentricity. Thus the real question is what kind of union security device should be adopted.

We reject the alternative of a "fair share" deduction for three reasons. First, it assumes that what unions do outside the narrow confines of negotiation and contract administration is somehow separable from and extraneous to its role as a collective bargaining agent. However, activities carried on before the executive and legislative branches to secure funding for the bargain struck, or to gather support of, or opposition to, other legislative matters directly affecting the public university—even to the point of supporting the election of friendly legislators— are clearly closely intertwined with and inseparable from the bargaining agent's role as a bargaining agent. Thus the distinction drawn by statutory fair-share provisions is theoretically unsound. Second, there are most arcane accounting problems in apportioning the costs of a host of union activities to the limited role this approach conceives for it as negotiator and contract administrator for the particular unit, for example, the costs of regional or national press relations and publications, costs of speaking engagements for local, regional, or national officers, overhead of the national headquarters, costs of the national convention, and so on. The almost exquisite distinctions compelled place in question the practicality of the fair-share assumption. Finally, a fair-share provision alone will not accommodate the conscientious objector who is opposed to any and all union activity.

If, as we have concluded, an agency shop is of benefit to the employer, the bargaining agent, and, in the longer run, the members of the bargaining unit, should it be merely a subject of bargaining or should it, as in Connecticut, be automatic upon the election of a bargaining agent? One argument against a statutorily mandated agency shop is that it creates a windfall for the bargaining agent. As a result organizations may be tempted to organize where they otherwise might not, or to spend larger amounts in an organizational campaign, because the funds will be easily recovered if victory is secured. If the election is affected by the size of such expenditures then an automatic deduction may conduce toward the election of the best capitalized. However, to the extent poorly capitalized organizations are encouraged to offer themselves, a wider electoral choice would be presented. A second and perhaps more persuasive argument is that by mandating an agency shop no requirement is placed on the bargaining agent to justify the amount exacted save by its own internal political processes. As a result it becomes increasingly likely that undesirable legislative or administrative controls will be imposed on the amount of the agency fee or its uses similar to those involved in the administration of the mandatory "fair share" statutes. While the arguments are almost equally persuasive, on balance we believe it preferable to allow the public employer and the bargaining agent to work out, by agreement, the terms and conditions of the agency shop, as in private employment—subject to certain conditions, including a conscientious objector provision.

While we follow the private sector model, we suggest that two provisions of the National Labor Relations Act not be imitated. The first is the requirement for individually signed authorization cards for the deduction of an agency shop fee from an employee's pay. A dues deduction authorization may be desirable where the parties do not agree on an agency shop; in that case, the payment of union dues is genuinely voluntary and the deduction is a convenience to the individual as well as of benefit to the union. In the presence of a union or agency shop, the requirement for a check-off authorization preserves only the right of an employee to pay dues by hand, rather than by check-off, a right of dubious value that can, in fact, prove to be a trap for the unwary and lead to being discharged, as it was in *Motor Coach Employees* v. *Lockridge*.[196] The second is the mandatory 30-day grace period (7 days for building and construction work). In the national act this prohibits the closed shop, that is, an arrangement under which only union members can be hired, while permitting the union shop, that is, an arrangement by which employees must join the union at some time after they are hired. Since our proposal does not permit any requirement of membership, the grace period would serve no useful purpose.

While we believe that a permissible union or agency shop, coupled with an exemption for conscientious objectors, is a satisfactory approach, policing the exemption does pose some problems. The agent could simply exempt any person who claims to be a conscientious objector. This approach, while easy to administer, holds

[196]403 U.S. 274 (1971).

open the possibility that large numbers will assert objector status out of economic motivation. Alternatively, the agent could establish some hearing procedure to ascertain the bona fides of a claim; this, however, would be most difficult to administer. The Montana Act, for example, establishes a hearing procedure to determine whether the protestant may appropriately claim exemption on the religious grounds provided in the Act. Accordingly, we propose that the statute require that any person claiming a conscientious objection be exempted automatically but permit the parties, by agreement, to compel the objector to pay a like amount to charity in lieu of dues. To be sure, the objector might make the same contribution to charity he otherwise would have made. Nevertheless, it removes some of the economic incentive to claim objector status while remaining relatively easy to police. In any event, it is up to the parties to tailor the exemption as they see fit. The following is phrased in terms applicable to public employees generally, but it could be narrowed for higher education.

RECOMMENDED PROVISION 8

Nothing in this statute, or any other statute of this state, shall preclude a public employer from making an agreement with a labor organization (not established, maintained, or assisted by any unfair labor practice) providing for the deduction from the wages of employees, and the payment to the labor organization, of amounts no greater than the periodic dues, initiation fees, and assessments uniformly required as a condition of acquiring or retaining membership if (1) such labor organization is the representative of the employees, as provided in this statute, (2) membership in such labor organization is available to any employee from whose wages such deductions are made on the same terms and conditions generally applicable to other members, and (3) provision is made for the exemption of any employee from such deductions on the grounds of conscientious objection to the payment of dues or fees to any labor organization, which exemption may be conditioned upon the payment by the exempted employee to any nonreligious charity or charities of amounts no greater than the deductions that would otherwise be made.

4

Tabular Summaries of Statutory Provisions

The following tables summarize statutory provisions on the two issues of utmost concern to faculty in higher education—unit determination criteria and scope of bargaining. Because it is exceedingly difficult to do justice to the subtleties of legislative draftmanship in phrasing a summary heading, we have appended notes clarifying the statute or its application.

Table 1. Criteria for bargaining unit determination

	Community of interest or a policy effectuating the right of self-organization	Geographical separation	History or extent of organization	Efficiency of administration	Level of government responsible for fiscal implementation	Desires of employees or recommendations of parties	Professionals vote on inclusion in unit with non-professionals	Supervisory (S) or managerial (M) employees excluded from bargaining	Separate bargaining unit provision for supervisory (S) or managerial (M) employees	Policy against fragmentation or favoring large units	States operating multicampus systems	Multicampus unit determined appropriate	Separate campus units determined appropriate
Alaska	x		x			x				x	x	x[a]	
Connecticut	x						x			x[b]	x	x	
Delaware	x		x										
Florida	x		x	x	x	x	x	M				x	x
Hawaii								M	S[c]	x[d]	x	x	
Iowa	x	x	x	x		x	x	S,M			x		no determination
Kansas	x	x	x	x		x		S,M			x	x	x
Maine									S[c]	x[e]	x		
Massachusetts	x		x				x	M			x		x[f]
Michigan	x							S					
Minnesota	x	x	x[g]			x[g]			S[h]		x	x[i]	x[i]
Montana	x		x			x		S,M			x		x
Nebraska	x[j]										x		x[k]
New Hampshire	x		x				x		S		x		x
New Jersey	x						x	M	S[l]		x	x	
New York	x		x	x				M			x	x	
Oregon	x[m]		x			x			S		x		x
Pennsylvania	x						x	M	S[n]	x[o]	x	x	
Rhode Island	x										x		x
South Dakota		x	x	x		x					x		no determination
Vermont	x	x	x					M			x	x	x

Notes to Table 1

[a]Alaska, like Hawaii, maintains a system combining the university with community colleges. However, by agreement the community colleges constitute a separate bargaining unit. On the other hand, the Alaska Labor Relations Agency declined to allow one of the four-year colleges in the system to constitute an appropriate unit. Alaska LRA Order No. 25 (July 26, 1976).

[b] Connecticut has established legislatively separate units for the faculties of the University of Connecticut, the state colleges, the state technical colleges, and the state vocational schools. Nonfaculty professional staff may be included by mutual agreement.

[c] The Hawaii and Maine provisions concerning supervisors do not affect faculty in higher education.

[d] The Hawaii Act establishes a single unit for the faculty of the university and the community colleges.

[e] Maine has legislatively established a faculty unit for the University of Maine system. Provision is made for the later establishment of modified systemwide units by the Maine Labor Relations Board.

[f] At the time the Massachusetts Act excluded salaries from the scope of bargaining, separate campus units for the state college system were determined to be appropriate, as was the Amherst campus of the University of Massachusetts. In a pending petition for representation for the university faculty no party seems to be urging separate campus units and most likely a single unit (exclusive of the medical school) will be decided to be appropriate.

[g] For state employees the Minnesota Act provides that all employees of the "appointing authority" shall compose a single bargaining unit unless professional, geographic, or other considerations clearly require some other composition. The unit criteria provided elsewhere in the Act give special weight to the history and extent of organization.

[h] A supervisor is excluded from rank-and-file units under the Minnesota Act only if he or she performs a majority of the functions that indicate supervisory status.

[i] The Minnesota Board held each of the campuses of the state college system to be a separate unit, which decision was reversed by the state's supreme court. The board has held each of the campuses of the University of Minnesota to be a separate unit.

[j] The Nebraska Act merely provides that the Court of Industrial Relations in determining the bargaining unit "shall consider established bargaining units and established policies of the employer." *Neb. Rev. Stat.* § 48-816 (1974).

[k] By consent the faculties of the four Nebraska state colleges compose a single unit. However, the Nebraska Court of Industrial Relations has determined that each campus of the university system comprises a separate unit.

[l] The New Jersey Act prohibits supervisors from being represented by an organization that admits nonsupervisors to membership unless the contrary is "dictated by established practice, prior agreement, or special circumstances." *N.J. Stat. Ann.* § 34:13A-5.3 (1976 Supp.).

[m] The Oregon Act explicitly provides that the labor board may decide a unit to be appropriate "even though some other unit might also be appropriate." *Ore. Rev. Stat.* § 243.682(1) (1975).

[n] Pennsylvania requires "first level" supervisors to be placed in separate bargaining units for which their representatives "meet and discuss," but not bargain "on matters deemed to be bargainable for other public employees." *Pa. Stat. Ann.* tit. 43 § 1101.704 (1976–1977 Supp.).

[o] While requiring the labor board to consider that the commonwealth as employer may be bargaining on a statewide basis, the Pennsylvania Act also provides that that provision "shall not be deemed to prohibit multi-unit bargaining." *Pa. Stat. Ann.* tit. 43 § 1101.604(4) (1976–1977 Supp.).

Table 2. Scope of bargaining

	Specific additions	Specific exclusions	Reservation of manage- ment rights	"Meet and dis- cuss" on agency policy
Alaska	Fringe benefits		x^a	
Florida			x^b	
Hawaii		Retirement benefits, any infringement of management rights	x^c	x^d
Iowa	x^e	Public employee retirement system, statutory duties of the public employer	x^f	
Kansas	x^g		x^h	
Massachusetts	Standards of productivity and performance			
Minnesota	Fringe benefits	Retirement contributions or benefits	x^i	x^j
Montana	Fringe benefits		x^k	
New Hampshire			x^l	
New Jersey		Matters governed by any pension statute		
New York		Retirement benefits		
Pennsylvania		x^m	x^n	x^o
Vermont	x^p	Any matter prescribed or controlled by statute	x^q	

Notes to Table 2

Note: All statutes adopt the general formulation of "wages, hours, and terms and conditions of employment" and grievance procedures; some make minor variations on this basic theme. Only those 13 states with significant departures affecting faculty are noted.

[a] The Alaska statute defines "terms and conditions of employment" as including "personnel policies affecting working conditions" but excluding "general policies describing the function and purpose of a public employer." *Alaska Stat.* § 23.40.250(7) (1972).

[b] The Florida Act provides that, "It is the right of the public employer to determine unilaterally the purpose of each of its constituent agencies, set standards of services to be offered to the public, and exercise control and discretion over its organization and operations. It is also the right of the public employer to direct its employees, take disciplinary action for proper cause, and relieve its employees duty because of lack of work or for other legitimate reasons," provided that the exercise of these rights shall not preclude the raising of grievances under collective bargaining agreements. *Fla. Stat. Ann.* § 447.005 (1976 Supp.).

[c] Hawaii excludes from bargaining any proposal that would "interfere with the rights of a public employer to (1) direct employees; (2) determine qualification, standards for work, the nature and contents of examinations, hire, promote, transfer, assign, and retain employees in positions and suspend, demote, discharge, or take other disciplinary action against employees for proper cause; (3) relieve an employee from duties because of lack of work or other legitimate rea-

son; (4) maintain efficiency of government operations; (5) determine methods, means, and personnel by which the employer's operations are to be conducted; and take such actions as may be necessary to carry out the missions of the employer in cases of emergencies." *Hawaii Rev. Stat.* § 89-9(d) (1975 Supp.).

^dBefore changes in "any major policy affecting employee relations" the employer is to make every reasonable effort to consult the collective representative. All matters affecting employee relations are subject to consultation. *Hawaii Rev. Stat.* § 89-9(c) (1975 Supp.).

^eThe Iowa Act omits "terms and conditions of employment" and supplies instead an extensive list of bargainable matters: that is, "wages, hours, vacations, insurance, holidays, leaves of absence, shift differentials, overtime compensation, supplemental pay, seniority, transfer procedures, job classifications, health and safety matters, evaluation procedures, procedures for staff reduction, in service training and other matters mutually agreed upon." *Iowa Code Ann.* § 20.9 (1976 Supp.).

^fThe Iowa Act provides that, in addition to all rights, powers, and duties established elsewhere in state law, public employers shall have the exclusive power, duty, and right to:
"1. Direct the work of its public employees.
2. Hire, promote, demote, transfer, assign, and retain public employees in positions within the public agency.
3. Suspend or discharge public employees for proper cause.
4. Maintain the efficiency of governmental operations.
5. Relieve public employees from duties because of lack of work or for other legitimate reasons.
6. Determine and implement methods, means, assignments and personnel by which the public employer's operations are to be conducted.
7. Take such actions as may be necessary to carry out the mission of the public employer.
8. Initiate, prepare, certify, and administer its budget.
9. Exercise all powers and duties granted to the public employer by law." *Iowa Code Ann.* § 20.7 (1976 Supp.).

^gThe Kansas Act supplies a definition of "conditions of employment" as "salaries, wages, hours of work, vacation allowances, sick and injury leave, number of holidays, retirement benefits, insurance benefits, wearing apparel, premium pay of overtime, shift differential pay, jury duty and grievance procedures, but nothing in this act shall authorize the adjustment or change of such matters which have been fixed by statute or by the constitution of this state." *Kan. Stat. Ann.* § 75-4322(t) (1975 Supp.).

^hKansas prohibits a collective agreement from trenching on the rights of the public employer. *Kan. Stat. Ann.* § 75-4330 (1975 Supp.). The rights of the public employee are defined in § 75-4326:
"Nothing in this act is intended to circumscribe or modify the existing right of a public employer to:
(a) Direct the work of its employees;
(b) Hire, promote, demote, transfer, assign and retain employees as parties within the public agency;
(c) Suspend or discharge employees for proper cause;
(d) Maintain the efficiency of governmental operations;
(e) Relieve employees from duties because of lack of work or for other legitimate reasons;
(f) Take actions as may be necessary to carry out the mission of the agency in emergencies; and
(g) Determine the methods, means and personnel by which operations are to be carried on."

ⁱThe Minnesota Act provides that a public employer "is not required to meet and negotiate on matters of inherent managerial policy, which include, but are not limited to, such areas of discretion or policy as the function and programs of the employer, its overall budget, utilization of technology, the organizational structure and selection and direction and number of personnel." *Minn. Stat.* § 179.66(1) (1976 Supp.).

^jThe obligation is imposed to "meet and confer with professional employees to discuss policies and those matters relating to their employment" not included in the scope of bargaining. *Minn. Stat.* § 176.66(3) (1976 Supp.).

^kThe Montana Act provides that public employee representatives "shall recognize the prerogatives of public employers to operate and manage their affairs." *Mont. Rev. Codes Ann.* § 54-1603(2) (1975 Cum. Supp.). The enumeration differs slightly from that in Hawaii and Iowa.

^lThe scope of bargaining in New Hampshire excludes "managerial policy within the exclusive prerogative of the public employer," *N.H. Rev. Stat.* § 273-A:1(X) (1975), which include the "functions, programs and methods of the public

employer, including the use of technology, the public employer's organizational structure, and the selection, direction and number of its personnel, so as to continue public control of governmental functions."

[m] The Act forbids the effectuation or implementation of any provision in a collective bargaining agreement "in violation of, or inconsistent with, or in conflict with" any state statute. *Pa. Stat. Ann.* tit. 43 § 1101.703 (1976–1977 Supp.)

[n] The employer is "not required to bargain over matters of inherent managerial policy," defined similarly to the Minnesota and New Hampshire provisions. *Pa. Stat. Ann.* tit. 43 § 1101.702 (1976–1977 Supp.).

[o] Public employers are required to "meet and discuss policy matters affecting wages, hours and terms and conditions of employment as well as the impact thereon upon request by public employee representatives." *Pa. Stat. Ann.* tit. 43 § 1101.702 (1976–1977 Supp.).

[p] Under 3 *Vt. Stat. Ann.* § 304(a) (1975 Supp.), all matters relating to the relationship between the employer and employee are bargainable, unless controlled or prescribed by statute, including

"(1) wage and salary schedules to the extent they are inconsistent with rates prevailing in commerce and industry for comparable work within the state;

(2) work schedules relating to assigned hours and days of the week;

(3) use of vacation or sick leave;

(4) general working conditions;

(5) overtime practices;

(6) rules and regulations for personnel administration, except the following: rules and regulations relating to persons exempt from the classified service and rules and regulations relating to applicants for the employment in state service and employees in an initial probationary status including any extension or extensions thereof provided such rules and regulations are not discriminatory by reason of an applicant's race, color, creed, sex or national origin."

[q] Under 3 *Vt. Stat. Ann.* § 905 (1975 Supp.), nothing in the statute is to "interfere with the right of the employer to:

(1) Carry out the statutory mandate and goals of the agency, or of the colleges, and to utilize personnel, methods and means in the most appropriate manner possible.

(2) With the approval of the governor, take whatever action may be necessary to carry out the mission of the agency in an emergency situation."

Index